# Selected Chapters from
## Data Analysis, Regression, and Forecasting
## &
## Risk Management

Arthur Schleifer, Jr. / David E. Bell
Harvard Business School, Boston, MA

**BROOKS/COLE**

TM

**THOMSON LEARNING**

COPYRIGHT © 2002 by the Wadsworth Group. Brooks/Cole is an imprint of the Wadsworth Group, a division of Thomson Learning Inc. Thomson Learning™ is a trademark used herein under license.

Printed in the United States of America

**Brooks.Cole**
**511 Forest Lodge Road**
**Pacific Grove, CA 93950**
**USA**

For information about our products, contact us:
**Thomson Learning Academic Resource Center**
**1-800-423-0563**
http://www.brookcole.com

**International Headquarters**
Thomson Learning
International Division
290 Harbor Drive, 2$^{nd}$ Floor
Stamford, CT 06902-7477
USA

**UK/Europe/Middle East/South Africa**
Thomson Learning
Berkshire House
168-173 High Holborn
London WCIV 7AA

**Asia**
Thomson Learning
60 Albert Street, #15-01
Albert Complex
Singapore 189969

**Canada**
Nelson Thomson Learning
1120 Birchmount Road
Toronto, Ontario MIK 5G4
Canada
United Kingdom

ISBN 0-534-41641-1

The Adaptable Courseware Program consists of products and additions to existing Brooks/Cole products that are produced from camera-ready copy. Peer review, class testing, and accuracy are primarily the responsibility of the author(s).

# Custom Contents

# DATA ANALYSIS AND STATISTICAL DESCRIPTION

## SOURCES AND ARRANGEMENTS OF DATA

Managers acquire data in a variety of ways. They draw upon internal sources of data, such as accounting or management-information systems, and external sources, such as libraries, trade publications, the United States census, public-opinion polls, market research, and consulting organizations. Managers sometimes commission surveys of customers, or conduct experiments to provide data on the effects of some contemplated change in a production process or marketing technique.

Raw data come in various forms: words, pictures, sounds, computerized bits and bytes, and ordinary numbers. In order to perform the sorts of analyses described in this text, raw data must be converted into numbers,[1] and arranged in a table or set of tables. These arrangements are called **data structures**. By far the most common data structures consist of **observations** on one or more **variables**. If the observations consist of people or objects examined at a particular moment of time, the data are called **cross-sectional**. Examples of cross-sectional data include observations of people in which the variables are their annual expenditure on a product, their age, their education, and their gender; or observations of personal computers in which the variables are retail price, amount of memory, number and type of disk drives, and hard-disk capacity. By contrast, if the observations represent periods of time, the data are referred to as a **time series**. Examples of time series include yearly observations, in which the variables are measures of economic activity, such as gross national product, unemployment, and inflation; or monthly or quarterly observations, in which the variables are sales of a product, advertising expenditures, and price.

Spreadsheets provide very useful ways to record observations on a set of variables. By convention, each row of a spreadsheet usually represents an observation, and each column a variable. Each cell contains the numeric **value** of a variable on an observation.

Harvard Business School note 2-191-114. This note was prepared by Professor Arthur Schleifer, Jr.
Copyright © 1990 by the President and Fellows of Harvard College.

---

[1] Ways in which nonnumeric data can be recorded will be discussed later in this chapter.

# PURPOSES OF DATA ANALYSIS

Why do we analyze data? One reason is to condense a mass of data into **summary statistics** that succinctly characterize the observations and variables. This condensation is called **statistical description**. Measures of distribution (histograms and cumugrams), of centrality (means, medians, and modes), of location (fractiles), and of spread (standard deviations and ranges) constitute the primary outputs from statistical description.

Another reason for analyzing data is to examine the relationship between two or more variables. Usually, we want to know not only if a relationship exists, but how to quantify it. For example, we might want to know if product sales are related to advertising expenditures and, if so, how much sales levels tend to change with each additional advertising dollar. More ambitiously, we may want to determine what causes what. Does advertising affect product sales, do sales levels influence advertising expenditures, or does some other factor influence both sales and advertising levels? Finally, we may need to base decisions on the results of the analysis: to boost sales, should we lower price, increase advertising, or both? By how much?

Once we determine the relationships among variables, we can **forecast** the unknown value of one variable when the values of other variables are specified. For example, we could use a time series to forecast the future value of a product's sales based on a specified level of advertising. However, this forecast represents only an **estimate** or best guess, since the relationships obtained from a sample of data may not be the same as those obtained from much more data. For this reason, it is useful to calculate the probability of an estimate's accuracy using **statistical inference**, and then report this probability along with the estimate.

Subsequent chapters address forecasting and statistical inference, while this chapter serves as an introduction to data analysis. It focuses on statistical description and the kind of exploratory data analysis that should always precede the use of these more powerful and sophisticated methods.

# DESCRIPTION OF DATA SETS AVAILABLE FOR ANALYSIS

You should browse through the following data sets on your Data Diskette to become familiar with their contents, as they will be referred to frequently in this and subsequent chapters.

## Smoking and Death Rates [SMOKING.XLS]

A 1966 study of the effects of smoking and inhalation on death rates[2] tracked a number of people annually from late 1959 through September 30, 1963. For each year that a person remained in the study, his or her age, gender, smoking behavior (self-reported) and status (alive or dead) were recorded. Treating each person-year as an observation, there were 2,904,813 observations and 29,562 deaths.

What can you say about the effects of smoking, age, and gender on death rates?

Harvard Business School note 2-894-003. Description of Data Sets Available for Analysis. This note was prepared by Arthur Schleifer, Jr. Copyright © 1993 by the President and Fellows of Harvard College.

---

[2] E. Cuyler Hammond, "Smoking in Relation to the Death Rate of One Million Men and Women," *National Cancer Institute Monograph No. 19.*

### Forecasts of Consumer Price Index [CPI.XLS]

A number of econometric forecasting services provide forecasts of key macroeconomic indicators up to two years ahead. These forecasts are typically issued each quarter.

The file contains quarterly forecasts of the consumer price index[3] (CPI) made by Data Resources, Inc., (DRI) a prominent forecasting firm. Each forecast predicted what the CPI would be one year later. To facilitate comparison with actual values of the CPI, the time associated with a forecast is the time at which that value was predicted to occur, not the time at which the forecast was made. Thus the forecast value of 123.3 listed for 7201 (the first quarter of 1972) was actually made in the first quarter of 1971.

What can you say about the accuracy of DRI's forecasts? Do they predict inflation rates well?

### First-Year Harvard MBA Data [HBSMBA.XLS]

The file contains data on 667 first-year MBA students at Harvard Business School in the early 1970s, including grade information, section, age, college average, and test-score results. The variables are more completely described in the data file itself.

What can you say about the factors affecting performance in the first year?

# DESCRIPTION OF ONE VARIABLE

## ▼ Measures of Distribution

A variable takes on different values on different observations. These values can be grouped into brackets of equal width. The number of times each bracket occurs constitutes the variable's **frequency distribution**. The frequency distribution is depicted visually by a histogram or a cumugram.

### Histograms

In a **histogram**, the **relative frequency** of each bracket is plotted as a bar in a bar graph. Figure 1.1 shows these relative frequencies for the weights of 768 first-year students at Harvard Business School.[4] The frequencies signify the fraction of students that fall into each weight category.

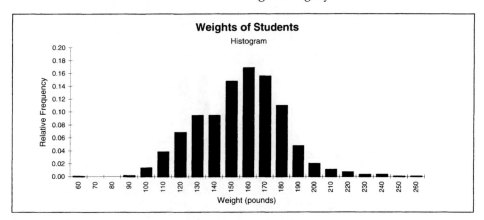

*Figure 1.1*

---

3 The index measures the price of a standard selection of consumer goods relative to a base price of 100 in 1967.

4 In a computer exercise conducted several years ago, students were asked, among other things, to supply their height (in inches), weight (in pounds), and gender. These variables are in file HTWT.XLS.

A first step in constructing such a histogram entails grouping the values into brackets. This step requires careful choices about the bracket width. If the brackets are too wide, disparate observations are grouped together. On the other hand, if the brackets are too narrow, each bar comprises very few observations, and the histogram is not likely to convey anything sensible about the shape of the distribution. In this example of HBS students, the weights are grouped into 10-pound brackets, and labeled such that the bracket denoted by 100 contains weights of at least 95 pounds but less than 105 pounds. For a discussion of how to produce histograms in Microsoft Excel 5.0, see the section called Worked Examples in Data Analysis Using Spreadsheets near the end of this chapter.

There are several important characteristics of a histogram. These include:

*Mode.*   The **mode** of a distribution corresponds to the highest bar in a histogram. It signifies the most frequently observed bracket. In Figure 1.1, the mode occurs at 160 pounds, i.e., for the bracket that extends from 155 to 164 pounds. In this example, the heights of the bars also decline steadily as you move away from the mode in either direction; the distribution is therefore called **unimodal**. By contrast, if the heights first decline as you move away from the highest bracket and then get higher again, the distribution is **multimodal**; when there are two peaks, it is **bimodal**.

*Symmetry.*   A distribution is **symmetric** when the bars on the right of the histogram mirror the bars on the left. An easy test for symmetry is to flip over the page containing the histogram and hold it up to the light; it is symmetric if its shape is pretty much like the shape of the original histogram. For example, the histogram in Figure 1.1 is fairly symmetric.

*Skewness.*   Distributions that are not symmetric are referred to as **skewed**. Figure 1.2 presents a histogram with a skewed distribution. In this case, the distribution is skewed to the right, since it has a long tail to the right. In the same vein, a distribution is skewed to the left if it has a long tail to the left.

**Figure 1.2**

*Multiplicative Symmetry.*   Sometimes a variable with a skewed distribution has a **multiplicatively symmetric distribution**. In the data from which Figure 1.2 was derived, 50% of the observations have values below $28,000, 7.5% have values below half of $28,000, or $14,000, and approximately 7.5% have values above twice $28,000, or $56,000. Taking the logarithm of these selling prices generates a fairly symmetric distribution, as shown in Figure 1.3.[5]

---

[5] See the final section of this chapter for a short discussion of logarithms and logarithmic graphs.

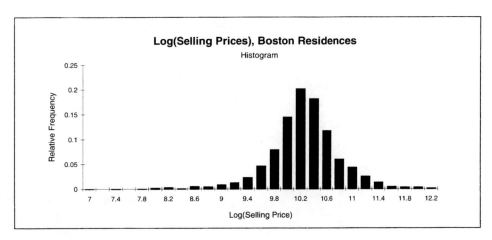

**Figure 1.3**

**Outliers.** In Figure 1.1, there is a barely visible bar corresponding to a bracket of 55-64 pounds, and no other bars until the 90-pound bracket. Both because it lies so far away from the other data and because this does not appear to be a reasonable weight for an HBS student, we might conjecture that this **outlier** was misreported and eliminate the observation.[6]

## Cumugrams

In contrast to histograms, plots of cumulative distributions, or **cumugrams**, use the individual values of a variable, without grouping into brackets. They show the fraction of values that are less than or equal to some particular value. Cumugrams assume that the values of a variable have a natural ordering, or that the relationships "less than" and "greater than" are meaningful. Figure 1.4 shows a cumugram of the student weight data. It shows that roughly 10% of the students weighed 120 pounds or less, and about half weighed 157 or less. The jaggedness of the cumugram in Figure 1.4 stems from the fact that many students rounded their weight to the nearest five pounds.

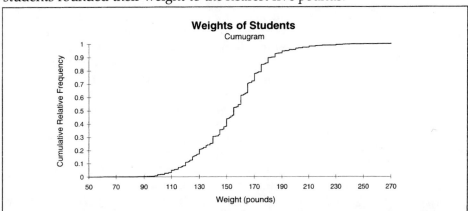

**Figure 1.4**

It is harder to detect modes and symmetry in cumugrams than in histograms. A mode occurs at a point of inflection in the cumugram where the graph stops increasing at an increasing rate and starts to increase at a decreasing rate. A cumugram is symmetric if its shape is about the same when viewed upside down as it is right-side up. In this way, you can verify that the cumugram in Figure 1.4 is roughly symmetric.

---

[6] If we check HTWT.XLS we see that the 60-pounder reported himself as 72" tall.

## ▼ Measures of Centrality

In describing a variable, we often want to specify a single value that is typical of the variable. Such a value is called a measure of **centrality** and indicates roughly where the middle of the distribution lies. The most common measures of centrality are the mode, the median, and the mean. We have already discussed the mode: it is the highest bar in the histogram. If the values are sorted, the **median** is the middle value: roughly half the values of the variable are less than the median and half are greater. In a cumugram, the median is the value on the horizontal axis that corresponds to a value of 0.5 on the vertical axis.[7] The **mean** of a variable is simply the average of its values, or the sum of its values divided by the number of values.[8]

In a symmetric distribution, the mode, median, and mean coincide. However, in a distribution that is skewed to the right, such as the one in Figure 1.2, the mode is less than the median, which is in turn less than the mean. By contrast, in a distribution that is skewed to the left, the mode is greater than the median, which is greater than the mean. The three measures of centrality for the student weight data and the Boston selling-price data are as shown in Table 1.1.

**Table 1.1**

|  | MODE | MEDIAN | MEAN |
|---|---|---|---|
| STUDENT WEIGHTS | 155-164 | 155 | 154.2 |
| BOSTON SELLING PRICES | $25,000-$29,999 | $28,000 | $32,809 |

The relationships among the mode, median, and mean indicate that the weight data are fairly symmetric, while the price data are clearly skewed.

These three measures of centrality have different sensitivities to a variable's distribution and units of measurement. The mode is perhaps most subject to the way the data are measured, and therefore least typical. For example, if students' weights are recorded to the nearest five pounds, the mode may be substantially different from the mode we would observe if weights were recorded to the nearest ten pounds; if weights were recorded to the nearest ounce, there might be no mode at all since every student might have a different recorded weight. By contrast, the mean is sensitive to extreme values of a variable. For example, if you were reporting starting salaries of 100 students graduating from college, and one of the students signed as a professional basketball player with a starting salary of $1 million, the mean might be a distorted measure of centrality. For its part, the median is not sensitive to extreme values, but for this reason fails to capture such variation in the data.

The choice between the mean and the median is often a matter of judgment, as the following example illustrates. Two groups of workers with comparable skills and job requirements receive the salaries shown in Table 1.2.

Both groups have the same median salary of $30,000. However, a quick glance at the data reveals that Group A receives substantially lower salaries than Group B: the means of $25,000 and $37,200, respectively, more accurately convey the differences between the two groups.

**Table 1.2**

| GROUP A | GROUP B |
|---|---|
| $15,000 | $25,000 |
| $16,000 | $26,000 |
| $30,000 | $30,000 |
| $31,000 | $45,000 |
| $33,000 | $60,000 |

---

[7] If the values of a variable are listed in a column of a spreadsheet, you can find the median by sorting the values and finding the value in the middle of the sorted list. The =MEDIAN() function in Excel finds the median value for you.

[8] The mean is easily computed in Excel using the =AVERAGE() function.

The Appendix to this chapter shows how the mode, median, and mean can each be thought of as a measure that is the best solution for a particular decision problem.

## ▼ Measures of Location

**Fractiles** serve as a measure of location. They represent the lowest value of a variable below which some specified fraction of the observations lie.[9] Any fractile can be found from a cumugram or a sorted list of the values. For example, you can use a cumugram to find the 0.75 fractile by locating 0.75 on the vertical axis, and then reading over to the curve and down to the horizontal axis. You should verify from the weight data in Figure 1.4 that the 0.75 fractile is approximately 170 pounds. Alternatively, you can locate the 0.75 fractile by sorting the values of the variable and then finding a value below which three-quarters of the observations lie. The median is the same as the 0.50 fractile.

## ▼ Measures of Spread

In analyzing a set of observations, we are often interested in knowing how the values of the variable spread out. Do they cluster tightly around the central value, or do their values vary widely? Several measures report the **spread**, or dispersion, of a variable's values.

*Standard Deviation.*   The standard deviation is the most widely used measure of spread. It measures the dispersion of values around the mean of a variable. It is computed by first determining the "deviations," or differences, between each value of a variable and the mean of the variable, then squaring these deviations, finding their average, and taking the square root of this average. More succinctly, the standard deviation is the square root of the average of the squared deviations.[10]

In general, the closer the observations are to the mean, the smaller is the standard deviation. The process of squaring the deviations accentuates values that are far from the mean.

*Range.*   The range also reports the spread of a variable. It simply measures the difference between the highest and lowest values of the variable. It should be used with caution, however, because it is strongly affected by outliers or, if the data consist of a sample, by the chances that a particular observation will be included in or excluded from the sample.

*Interquartile Range.*   Still another useful measure of spread is the interquartile range. This measures the difference between the 0.75 and the 0.25 fractiles, a range that contains half the observations.

## ▼ Types of Variables

Good data analysis depends on recognizing that the measures of distribution, centrality, location, and spread that can be used in summarizing a variable depend on that variable's type, or scale of measurement.

---

[9] Fractiles and percentiles essentially measure the same thing: the 0.75 fractile is the 75th percentile, for example. Occasionally, the definition of percentile is reversed: depending on context, an exam grade in the 5th percentile may be in the upper 5% or lower 5% of all grades given.

[10] In Excel the =STDEVP() function computes the standard deviation.

***Ratio-scale variables.***   A variable is measured on a **ratio scale** if its values have no natural upper bound and cannot be negative. Dollar or unit sales, dividends, interest rates, inventories, number of employees, gross national product, salaries, prices, and time needed to perform a task are examples of ratio-scale variables. All the measures introduced above can be used to describe ratio-scale variables.

***Difference-scale variables.***   A variable is measured on a **difference scale** if its values can be either positive or negative, with no natural upper or lower bound. Profits, inflation rates, a budget surplus or deficit, trade balances, and growth rates are all difference-scale variables. All the measures of distribution, centrality, location, and spread can also be used to describe difference-scale variables. However, they differ from ratio-scale variables in one important way. Since the variables may take on positive or negative values, it is sometimes inappropriate to use ratios and percentage changes to discuss difference-scale variables. Even though many people would characterize an increase in profits from $10 to $15 million as a 50% increase, that kind of characterization works only when both the starting and ending values are positive, and even so may be a poor descriptive measure. Is a 200% increase in profit from $100 thousand to $300 thousand better or worse than the aforementioned increase?

***Ordinal variables.***   **Ordinal** variables are also numeric, but while "greater than" and "less than" relations are meaningful, differences between values are not. Questionnaires sometimes ask people whether they "strongly disagree, disagree, neither agree nor disagree, agree, or strongly agree" with a statement. If the five possible responses are coded 1 through 5, then the higher a person's numeric value, the more he or she agrees with the question. Nevertheless, the difference between a 3 and a 4 is not necessarily the same as the difference between a 4 and a 5 for a given individual, nor is the difference between a 3 and a 5 necessarily twice as great as the difference between a 4 and a 5.

Because the numerical differences between ordinal numbers are not equal, the mean and standard deviation are, strictly speaking, inappropriate measures. Nonetheless, the mean may convey more about the data than the median. If a group of five respondents replied to one question with coded responses of 1, 1, 3, 4, 4, and to another question with 2, 2, 3, 5, 5, the mean probably tells you more about the difference in the group's reactions to the two questions than the median. Similarly, the standard deviation may provide a better description of spread than strictly correct measures.

***Categorical variables.***   **Categorical** variables consist of both qualitative variables—such as religion and marital status—and numeric labels—such as SIC (standard industrial classification) codes, Social Security numbers, part numbers, and zip codes. Differences, relations of "less than" or "greater than," and ratios have no meaning for categorical variables. For example, there is no meaningful interpretation to the statement that my zip code is 47% higher than yours, or 1,750 higher than yours, or even higher than yours. For this reason, cumugrams, means, medians, and fractiles are not suitable summary measures for categorical variables, although histograms are appropriate.

***Dummy variables.***   A special case occurs when we are considering categorical variables with just two values, such as male vs. female, or married vs. single, or bankrupt vs. solvent, or pass vs. fail. By convention, these variables are coded so that one of the numerical values is a 0 and the other is a 1; the numerical value assigned to each category is completely arbitrary. Since "less than" and "greater than" have no meaningful interpretations, fractiles and medians are not applicable measures. However, the mode and mean are meaningful: the mode reveals which category occurs with higher frequency; and the mean is the fraction of observations in the data that are coded as 1. A dummy variable's standard deviation can be calculated in the usual way, but it also can be expressed as a formula, $\sqrt{f * (1 - f)}$ , where $f$ is the fraction of 1s, i.e., the mean of the dummy variable. No matter what the value of $f$, the standard deviation of a dummy variable cannot exceed 0.5.

Table 1.3 lists the key characteristics of, and measures that are applicable to and inappropriate for, each type of variable.

**Table 1.3**

**Key Characteristics of Variable Types**

| TYPE OF VARIABLE | CHARACTERISTICS | EXAMPLES | MEASURES THAT DON'T APPLY |
|---|---|---|---|
| Ratio-scale | Positive, no upper bound | Prices, GNP, # of employees | |
| Difference-scale | Positive or negative, no upper or lower bound | Profits, growth rates | Percentage change* |
| Ordinal | Numeric variable, "ordered" | Class rank, responses on scale of 1 to 5 | Mean,* standard deviation,* percentage change |
| Categorical | Qualitative variables and numeric labels | Marital status, religion, SS#, zip codes | Fractiles, cumugram, median, mean, percentage change |
| Dummy | Two-valued qualitative variables whose values are coded 0 or 1 | Political party affiliation, gender, yes/no | Fractiles, median, percentage change |

* Sometimes, although not strictly correct, these measures may summarize variables more effectively than any others.

# DESCRIPTION OF TWO OR MORE VARIABLES

## Independent and Dependent Variables and the Question of Causation

In many analyses, we are particularly interested in how the value of one variable changes when the value of one or more other variables changes. How do sales of a product change when advertising and price change? What is the effect of education, experience, seniority, and special skills on employees' salaries in an organization? How are motor-vehicle accident rates in various states affected by alcohol consumption, speed limits, amount of driving, and motor-vehicle inspection requirements? In all of these cases, there is one variable (sales, salaries, accident rates) whose variability we are trying to understand or explain. This is commonly called the **dependent variable**.

At the same time there are a number of other variables, changes in whose values are accompanied by changes in the value of the dependent variable. These variables are usually called **independent**, or **explanatory**, **variables**.

When we observe that the value of the dependent variable changes as the value of an independent variable changes, we sometimes use the language of causation to describe this relationship. We say, for example, that the independent variables (e.g., advertising and price) *affect* the dependent variable (e.g., sales), or that the *effect* of a $1 per unit decrease in price is to increase sales by 1,000 units per month. Because the language is so suggestive, it is easy to fall into the trap of assuming that this observed statistical association between variables is evidence of causation: that if we reduced price by $1, sales would necessarily increase by 1,000 units per month on the average. Some statistics texts caution against ever inferring causation based on the relationships among variables in observational (nonexperimental) data. It is easy to be misled. For example, suppose that the greater the number of police per capita in U.S. cities, the higher the violent crime rate, on average. Should we conclude that police cause crime?

By refusing to make any causal inferences on the basis of observational data you can avoid making blunders, but at a great cost. Managers, policy makers, and individuals do look at relationships in past data to try to learn what variables affect some particular variable of interest, and by how much. Managers of retail stores and fast-food establishments decide where to locate new stores on the basis of statistics showing the relationship between various characteristics of existing sites and the success of the stores located on them. Legislators enact vehicle-inspection laws based on statistics showing a relationship between inspection requirements and motor-vehicle death rates. Informed smokers try to decide whether to give up smoking based on statistics showing a relationship between smoking and death rates. The leap from "effects" observed in data to causal effects is a large one. In the remainder of this chapter and in subsequent chapters we discuss pitfalls to be wary of, and methods of acquiring and analyzing data that enhance the chances of your making reasonable causal inferences from the data.

## Scatter Diagrams

One way to see how one variable varies with another is to plot a **scatter diagram**. Possible values of an independent variable $(x)$ are displayed on the horizontal axis, and possible values of the dependent variable $(y)$ on the vertical axis. Each point corresponds to the values of the dependent and independent variables on an observation. Figure 1.5 shows weight as the dependent variable and height as the independent variable for the student data discussed previously. The diagram shows that weight tends to increase as height increases, that the overall relationship between weight and height could be represented by a straight or slightly curved line, and that there would be a great deal of scatter around such a line.

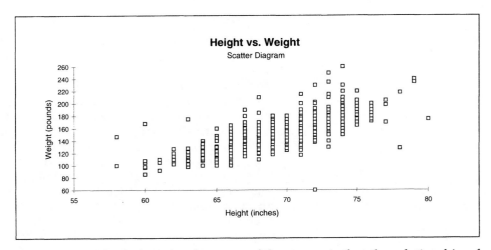

**Figure 1.5**

One possible explanation for some of the scatter is that the relationship of weight to height may be different for women than for men. Suppose women of a given height weigh less, on the average, than men of the same height. Then the overall relationship between women's weights and heights might be represented by a line or curve below the corresponding curve for men, and this in itself could account for some of the scatter. To explore this hypothesis, we could look at separate scatter diagrams for men and for women, but all of the information can be conveyed on a single diagram in which points for men are represented by a different symbol than points for women. Figure 1.6 shows a scatter diagram identical to that of Figure 1.5, except that each point identifies the person's gender (a circle for women; a square for men). Although there is much overlap, the diagram shows that women tend to cluster to the lower left (shorter and lighter), and for any given height, women tend to weigh less than men. This confirms the hypothesis we started with, and accounts in a small but important way for some of the scatter. Using an **identifier** to represent values, or brackets of values, of a second independent variable in a scatter diagram is often a useful diagnostic tool.

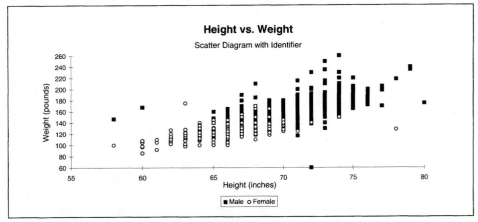

**Figure 1.6**

Of course, considerable scatter remains. Some of it may be explained in terms of other variables (heights and weights of parents, health, nutrition, ethnicity), and some may be unexplainable or random. Even if we had the data on additional potential explanatory variables, however, we would have trouble graphing their joint effects: we must wait for more powerful analytic tools.

## Correlation

When high values of one variable accompany high values of another variable and, similarly, when low values accompany low values, the variables are positively correlated. As an example, companies with a large number of employees also tend to have large asset bases, while those with relatively few employees tend to have smaller asset bases. There are of course exceptions, but if the relationship is true in general, we can say that number of employees and assets are **positively correlated**.

If high values of one variable accompany low values of another (and vice versa), the variables are **negatively correlated**. For example, low inflation tends to accompany high unemployment, and high inflation tends to accompany low unemployment; therefore, inflation and unemployment are negatively correlated.

Two variables that are positively correlated have a scatter diagram whose points cluster around an upward-sloping line that goes from southwest to northeast. Roughly speaking, the closer the points are to an upward-sloping (northeasterly sloping) line, the higher the correlation. The scatter diagram of weight vs. height (Figure 1.5) shows that weight and height are positively correlated. By contrast, a scatter diagram whose points cluster around a downward-sloping (southeasterly sloping) line indicates that the two variables are negatively correlated. In the case of a scatter diagram whose points cluster around a horizontal line, the two variables are uncorrelated with each other.

The **correlation coefficient** is a measure of correlation. To compute it, we first find the **covariance** between two variables, which is a measure of how $x$ and $y$ covary. Suppose we have $n$ observations on each of two variables, $x$ and $y$. Let $m_x$ be the mean of $x$ on the $n$ observations available, and similarly let $m_y$ be the mean of $y$. For each observation, compute the product $(x - m_x)*(y - m_y)$, and average these products. This average is called the **covariance**. If, on a particular observation, both $x$ and $y$ are above their respective means, the product for that observation will be positive. The same will be true when $x$ and $y$ are both below their respective means. If most of the observations have $x$ and $y$ values that are jointly above or jointly below their means, the covariance will tend to be positive. If, on the contrary, whenever $x$ is above its mean $y$ tends to be below its mean, and vice versa, the covariance will tend to be negative. The magnitude of the covariance depends on the variability of the $x$ values and the $y$ values, and the degree to which they vary together.

To find the **correlation coefficient**, we next divide the covariance by the product of the standard deviations of the two variables. The resulting number cannot exceed +1, nor be less than –1. A correlation coefficient of +1 represents a case where the points in a scatter diagram all lie exactly on an upward-sloping straight line; a coefficient of –1 represents a case where the points all lie on a downward-sloping straight line. The correlation coefficient for height vs. weight is +0.745.

The correlation coefficient is a useful way of describing the extent to which two variables are linearly related. It is a pairwise measure: if you have three variables, $x$, $y$, and $z$, you can compute the correlation between $x$ and $y$, between $x$ and $z$, and between $y$ and $z$. These pairwise correlations are often presented in a tabular form that is called a **correlation matrix**.[11] Table 1.4 gives a sample correlation matrix of height vs. weight. Since the correlation of $x$ vs. $y$ is the same as $y$ vs. $x$, a correlation matrix typically gives the correlation between a pair only once.

**Table 1.4** _____

|     | HT    | WT    |
| --- | ----- | ----- |
| HT  | 1.000 |       |
| WT  | 0.745 | 1.000 |

---

[11] The =CORREL() function in Excel will calculate the correlation between two variables.

As was true in our discussion of independent and dependent variables, high correlation between $x$ and $y$ does not necessarily mean that there is a causal relationship between $x$ and $y$. For example, high correlation between stock prices and house sales over time may be due wholly or in part to the fact that both tend to increase as interest rates decline, whether or not they are causally related.

## Simple Description of Effects

We observed in Figure 1.6 that height and weight are positively correlated and this relationship holds true for women as well as men. If we want to specify these relationships in a quantitative way, we could list the average weight of men in one-inch height increments, and do the same for women. The result would produce a lot of detail, but little understanding of the way weight is related to height. At the opposite extreme, we could assert that each additional inch of height is accompanied by an average of four additional pounds for both men and women, but that women of any given height weigh 25 pounds less, on the average, than men of the same height. This description conveys a large amount of information succinctly and simply.

If the relationships among height, weight, and gender were adequately summarized by the preceding assertion, we would call the relationship **linear** and **additive**. Because we assert that each one-inch increment in a man's or woman's height is accompanied by the same average increment in weight, whether the increment is from 62 to 63 inches or from 72 to 73 inches, the relationship between height and weight for either sex is graphed as a straight line: it is linear. Furthermore, for a man and a woman of the same height, the man's weight, on the average, is asserted to be 25 pounds greater than the woman's, regardless of whether the man and woman in question are both 62 inches tall or are both 72 inches tall. Under these assumptions, the effect of gender is additive.

While linear and additive descriptions of relationships are simple and intuitive, they are not necessarily right. Looking at the same data, one could instead assert that weight should increase with the cube of height, since height is a linear measure and weight a volume measure. Careful analysis of the data might reveal that this nonlinear relationship provides a better description. Alternatively, if the relationship between height and weight were linear, it might be that an additional inch of height increases weight for men by six pounds, and for women by only three pounds, on the average. In this case, the relationship between height and gender and weight would be linear but not additive.

The tradeoff between simplicity and more accurate description often comes down to a matter of judgment. Sometimes, as explained later in this chapter, we can transform a relationship that is neither linear nor additive into one that is both, and thus achieve a much simpler description.

## Time Series

In a **time series**, the observations are ordered chronologically and one of the independent variables may be time itself. When time is the only independent variable, the time series reveals the values of some dependent variable over time. As an illustration, Figure 1.7 on the following page displays monthly sales of all retail stores in the United States from June 1982 through February 1988.

**Figure 1.7**

The graph reveals two characteristics of this time series:

▶ There is a pronounced seasonal pattern: sales shoot up in December and then decline precipitously in January and February, before returning to a more normal level for the rest of the year.

▶ There is a steady upward trend: the December peaks are higher each year, and even the January-February troughs are generally higher; in between, the level also tends to increase with time.

***Trends and Seasonals.*** How can we capture the trend and seasonal effects graphically and display them more vividly? One simple device is to lay out a twelve-month scale on the horizontal axis and display individual line graphs for each year. This is done in Figure 1.8, which shows that each year's data moved higher on the graph, and that there was a pronounced seasonal pattern within each year. Would this display help you forecast retail sales for December 1988? Why or why not?

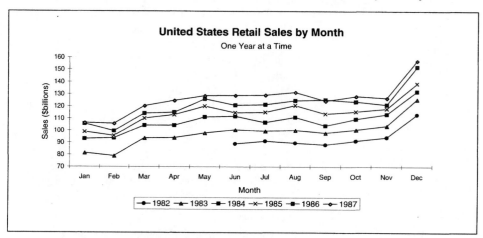

**Figure 1.8**

***Multiple Time Series.*** Often, when we are trying to understand the behavior of one time series, we introduce another time series to serve as an independent variable. In the retail sales example, we could introduce advertising expenditures over time as an independent variable to help explain how retail sales change over time. We might hypothesize that the stores' advertising expenditures generate sales. Figure 1.9 shows both retail sales and advertising as time series, with different scales for the two series.

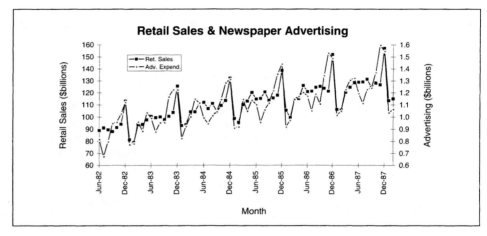

**Figure 1.9**

This graph shows that:

▶ Advertising expenditures constituted roughly 1% of retail sales dollars for the entire period.

▶ The seasonal pattern of advertising expenditures closely mirrors that of retail sales, except that advertising expenditures build up to the December peak more gradually, increasing more in October and November and less in December, than sales do.

***Deseasonalization.*** Because so much of the month-to-month fluctuation in retail sales is due to purely seasonal effects, it is common to report (and think about) sales on a deseasonalized basis. The fact that January sales are below the previous December's is not in itself cause for despair; what you would really like to know is the trend in deseasonalized sales. We shall learn later how to take seasonality into account in forecasting; for now, all you need to know is that retail sales and many other time series that exhibit strong seasonal effects are reported both in natural and in deseasonalized form. Figure 1.10 is a graph of deseasonalized sales. From that graph, you can more easily detect trends in the data.

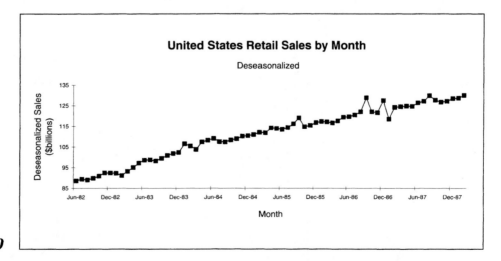

**Figure 1.10**

# AGE AS AN INDEPENDENT VARIABLE: LIFE-CYCLE VS. COHORT EFFECTS

Data about people (customers, employees, taxpayers, students, etc.) often include age as an independent variable. Markets are often segmented by age: consider sales of popular records, or air travel, or breakfast cereals, for example. Certain behavioral phenomena tend to be thought of as age-related: it is commonly believed that people tend to become more conservative politically as they grow older, for example. Other phenomena seem to depend on a particular generation's exposure to ideas or products: in the 1990s, young people tend to be more adept at using computers than older people. We might predict that a twenty-year-old person is likely to become more conservative politically in thirty years, but that her ability to use a computer will remain high when she turns fifty (and will be greater than that of most people who are currently fifty years old). If the general tendency for people to become more conservative politically as they age will be as clear twenty years from now as it is now, this phenomenon is called a **life-cycle effect**. If the computer ability of people who are currently young persists over their lifetime, this phenomenon is called a **cohort effect**. In interpreting cross-sectional data in which age or some variable related to age (experience, date of birth, year of graduation, seniority) has an important effect on some other variable, it is impossible to determine from the data alone whether the observed effect is a life-cycle or a cohort effect. Because misinterpretation of age-related variables is so common, it is useful to understand how easily one can be misled.

## An Example

In 1993 about 500 randomly selected alumni of a university were asked to describe their personal feeling of gratitude toward their school. Figure 1.11 shows the average score on a ten-point scale (with 1 low and 10 high) as a function of year of graduation. The figure shows that older alumni felt more gratitude, on average, than more recent graduates. Is this because whatever the university does to make alumni grateful was less effective in recent years than in the past (a cohort effect), or is it because graduates' feeling of gratitude grows as they age (a life-cycle effect)?

*Figure 1.11*

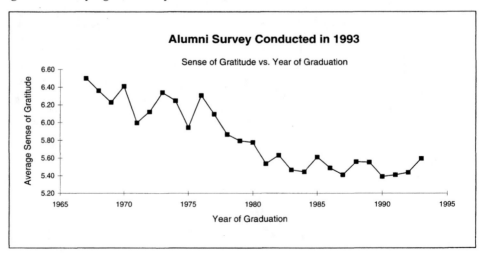

If gratitude of alumni is important to the university, then the university's administration should be concerned if the observed trend is a cohort effect, but should not be concerned if it is a life-cycle effect. There is no way of knowing from the data, however, which effect accounts for the trend, or whether it is the result of a combination of effects.

Suppose the identical survey were conducted again five years later, in 1998, and resulted in Figure 1.12, which for classes from 1967 through 1993 looks exactly like Figure 1.11. The evidence suggests that graduates of the class of 1993 remain as ungrateful in 1998 as they were in 1993, while graduates of the late 1960s and early 1970s continue to be as grateful: the effect is a cohort effect. If, on the other hand, the graph for the 1998 survey looked like Figure 1.13, we would attribute the observed trend to a life-cycle effect: in 1998 graduates of the class of 1998 have the same level of gratitude that graduates of the class of 1993 did in 1993; in 1998 graduates of the class of 1980 have the same level of gratitude that graduates of the class of 1975 did in 1993, etc. Of course, the 1998 graph might look different from either of these extremes, but we might find that it looked close enough to one of them to convince us that one of the two effects was more important.

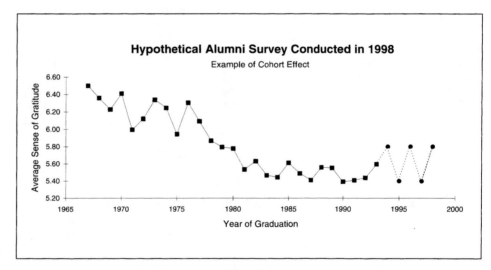

*Figure 1.12*

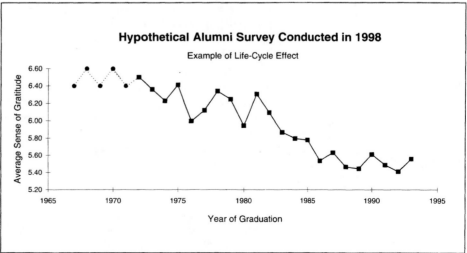

*Figure 1.13*

The moral of this example is that a single snapshot showing the relationship between age (or an equivalent variable) and some variable of interest is insufficient to sort out life-cycle vs. cohort effects. At least two such snapshots, separated in time, are needed.

# LOGARITHMS AND MULTIPLICATIVE EFFECTS

## Multiplicative Symmetry: A Second Look

In our discussion of histograms earlier in this chapter we showed that some variables have multiplicatively symmetric distributions. We stated, without any justification, that the logarithmic transformation of some variables has a distribution that exhibits ordinary symmetry. The reason for this is not hard to understand if you recall one key fact about logarithms: the logarithm of the product of two or more numbers is the sum of their logarithms. Thus, for example,

$$\log(a*b*c) = \log(a) + \log(b) + \log(c) \quad .$$

This is true whether you are using so-called natural logarithms (logarithms to the base $e$, where $e = 2.71828$, approximately), or logarithms to the base 10.[12] You should convince yourself, using a spreadsheet or a calculator, that

$$\log(2*3*4) = \log(2) + \log(3) + \log(4)$$

for both natural logarithms and logarithms to the base 10.

Distributions that are multiplicatively symmetric often arise when the value of each observation is the product of a number of small random effects. The logarithm of such a value will then be the sum of a number of small random effects and the distribution of such a set of values is likely to be symmetric. Thus, logarithms convert or **transform** multiplicative effects into additive effects.

## Multiplicative Seasonals and Constant Growth Rates

If you turn back to Figure 1.7, the graph of retail sales over time, you will notice that the amplitude of the swings between the December peak and the January-February trough seems to get larger over time. One possible explanation is that the seasonal effect is multiplicative. Suppose, for example, that every December tends to be 20% above normal and every January 15% below normal. Then the difference between December and January will be larger for high levels of sales, and smaller for low levels. Because the level of sales has been increasing over time, the differences will therefore get larger over time. If the seasonal effect of each month is, in fact, a constant multiple of some normal level of sales, then a graph showing a time series of the **logarithm** of sales will depict seasonal effects that add to or subtract from normal the same constant amount for each month: on the logarithmic scale, the seasonal effects will not change with the level of the series. Figure 1.14 shows such a graph; it seems to confirm the multiplicative-seasonal hypothesis.

---

[12] In Excel, =LN() calculates the natural logarithm and =LOG() the base-10 logarithm. On pocket calculators, the LN and LOG keys usually serve the same purposes, respectively.

**Figure 1.14**

A constant growth rate means that successive values in a time series are constant multiples of preceding values. For instance, if a variable increases by 5% per year, each year's value will be 1.05 times the preceding year's. If this is so, the logarithm of the values in the time series will have values that are constant **increments** above preceding values, and therefore a graph of the logarithmic series will have a shape close to a straight line. The U.S. population, the consumer price index, gross national product, and electric power generation all exhibit patterns of multiplicative growth over sufficiently long periods of time. The values increase at an increasing rate, often described as exponential growth. Figure 1.15, a graph of electric energy production in the United States from 1920 to 1983, exhibits this kind of exponential growth, at least through the mid-1970s. Figure 1.16, a graph of the logarithm of the series, is more nearly linear. Notice that by "linearizing" the series we can more easily detect the effects of the 1930s depression, the end of World War II, and the OPEC oil crisis of the 1970s on energy production.

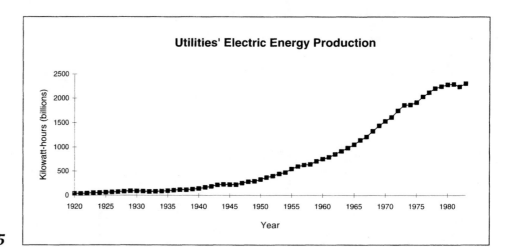

**Figure 1.15**

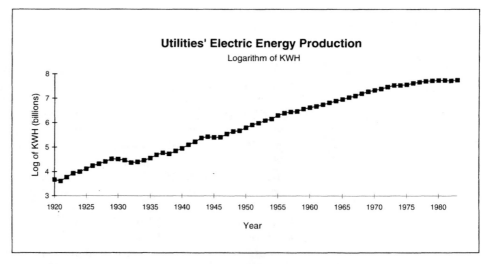

**Figure 1.16**

## Multiplicative Effects in Cross-Sectional Data

Even in cross-sectional data, the values of a variable may depend on the values of other variables in a multiplicative way. A company's salary structure may reward seniority and education, among other things. Suppose that in a given year starting salary for a person without a college education is $20,000, that college-educated employees earn 25% more than employees with comparable seniority, and that each year of seniority confers 5% more salary. Figure 1.17 shows what salaries would be if there were no additional factors affecting salary. Figure 1.18 shows the effects of seniority and education on log(salary). For a given level of seniority, education adds the same amount to log(salary), no matter what the level of seniority; we say that the effect of education on log(salary) is **multiplicative**. When we look at the effect of seniority on log(salary) for either level of education, we observe that it is linear, and this implies that the effect of seniority on salary is multiplicative.

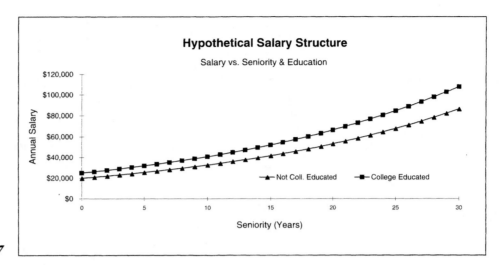

**Figure 1.17**

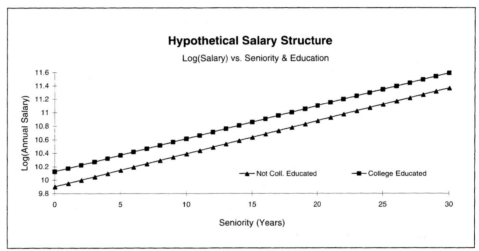

**Figure 1.18**

In general, when the relationship between two variables is not linear and the dependent variable is measured on a ratio scale, it is a good idea to see whether effects can be more simply explained by looking at graphs of the logarithm of the dependent variable. A logarithmic transformation of a ratio-scale dependent variable may:

▶ produce a symmetric, rather than a skewed, distribution of the dependent variable.

▶ produce a linear and additive relationship between the independent variables and the transformed dependent variable, if the effects on the natural dependent variable were multiplicative.

In performing transformations on our data, such as a log transform, we trade off complexity to get simplicity in the form of straight lines and additive effects.

## Graphs with Logarithmic Scales

Ordinary graphs are plotted on an arithmetic scale, so that each increment on an axis represents equal distance (i.e., the distance from 1 to 2 is the same as the distance from 2 to 3). Sometimes graphs are plotted on a ratio or logarithmic (log) scale, in which equal distances represent equal percent changes (i.e., the distance from 1 to 2 is the same as the distance from 2 to 4).

Figures 1.19A–C show three different ways of plotting monthly values of the Standard and Poors 500 Stock Index, from January 1968 through January 1993. Part A shows values of the Index on an arithmetic scale, B shows values of log (Index) on an arithmetic scale, and C shows values of the Index on a log scale.[13] Both B and C are essentially the same graphs: when you want to capture multiplicative effects of a ratio-scale variable graphically, graphs of either sort are equally appropriate.

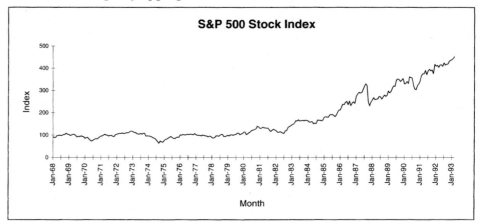

*Figure 1.19A*

*Figure 1.19B*

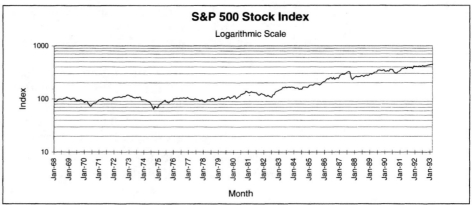

*Figure 1.19C*

---

[13] Excel permits you to create either line charts or XY (scatter) charts with logarithmic scales.

Notice that both the B and C graphs convey a great deal more information about stock-market fluctuations than does A. Looking at A, for example, it appears that the major stock-market declines occurred during the crash of 1987 and prior to the Gulf War in late 1990. Both B and C show, however, that the percentage decline from 1969 to 1970 was as severe as—though more protracted than—the 1987 crash, while the decline from late 1972 to late 1974 was substantially more severe than the crash.

# APPENDIX: MEASURES OF CENTRALITY AS SOLUTIONS TO DECISION PROBLEMS

It is instructive (and will prove useful in the context of regression) to think of the mode, median, and mean as solutions to decision problems involving finding the optimal value to represent all the values of a variable.

Consider the following fifteen observations on a variable: 1, 3, 4, 7, 7, 7, 8, 9, 12, 16, 19, 19, 25, 30, 37. Suppose you were asked to pick a particular number (not necessarily one corresponding to one of the observed values of the variable), after which one of these fifteen values would be picked at random. If you were penalized $1 if you were wrong, what number would you pick? You could draw the decision tree, but you can easily see that the number that minimizes your expected penalty is the one that occurred most frequently—the mode, or 7. You would have only 3 chances in 15 (20%) of avoiding the $1 penalty, but there is nothing that you could do that would improve your chances. The expected value of the penalty would be $0.80 if you picked 7, and would be higher if you picked any other number.

Now suppose that you were asked to pick a number, but were penalized $1 times the amount of your error. For instance, if you picked 7 and the number 3 were drawn at random, you would be penalized $4; if, instead, 30 had been picked at random, you would have been penalized $23. What number should you pick? This is a critical-fractile problem: if you think tentatively of picking a number, say 7, and then ask for the incremental gain or loss of picking 8 instead, you would *gain* $1 (relative to the penalty you would have incurred had you picked 7 instead) if the random draw were 8 or higher, but would *lose* $1 if the random draw were less than 8. The same incremental gains and losses would apply for any decision to add one to the number you had tentatively picked. Therefore, to minimize your expected penalty, you should pick the $G/(G + L) = 1/(1 + 1) = 0.50$ fractile, or the **median**, which in this case is 9. The expected value of the penalty would be $8/15 + 6/15 + 5/15 + 2/15 + 2/15 + 2/15 + 1/15 + 0/15 + 3/15 + 7/15 + 10/15 + 10/15 + 16/15 + 21/15 + 28/15 = 8.07$, and would be higher (or at least no lower) if you picked any other number.

Suppose that instead of being penalized $1 times the error, you were penalized $1 times the *square* of the error. If you picked 7 and the random draw were 3, you would be penalized $16, for example. It can be shown that under this penalty structure, you should pick the *mean*, or 13.6. You can compute the minimum expected penalty as 103.97.

The mode is the right number to pick if you avoid a penalty only if the random draw is exactly equal to your pick; the median is correct if the penalty is proportional to the error; and the mean is correct if the penalty is proportional to the square of the error. In this sense, the mean is said to be a **least-squares** estimate.

Figures 1.20,[14] 1.21, and 1.22 show the expected penalty as a function of the number picked for the three problems we have considered. The black dot shows the pick for which the expected penalty is minimized.

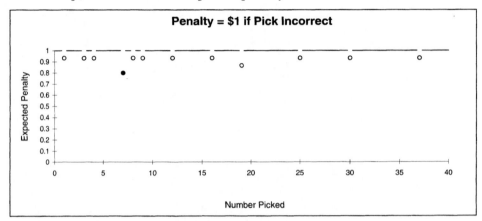

**Figure 1.20**

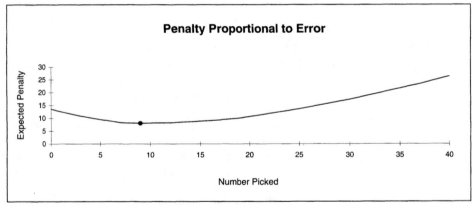

**Figure 1.21**

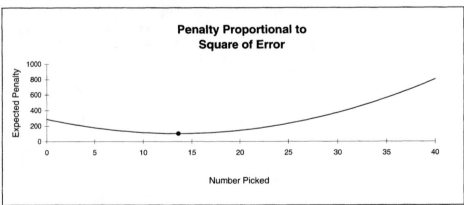

**Figure 1.22**

---

[14] The broken horizontal line at the value 1 in Figure 1.20 indicates that picking any number that is not one of the twelve values actually observed will result in a certain penalty of $1.

# EXERCISES ON INTERPRETING DATA [CHAP1EX.XLS]

QUESTION

**Who was the more valuable player, with respect to batting statistics, in 1991? How could Murray beat Merced both as a left-handed and a right-handed batter and still have a lower batting average?**

## Problem 1: Batting Averages

In 1991, Eddie Murray of the Los Angeles Dodgers and Orlando Merced of the Pittsburgh Pirates both played first base in baseball's National League. Murray and Merced were solid "switch hitters," which means they could bat either left-handed or right-handed.

A player's batting average (BA) is one of the most important statistics in baseball. The BA is calculated by dividing the number of hits by the number of plate appearances—or at bats. So a batter who gets a hit one out of every three times at the plate would have a BA of .333. When contracts are negotiated and player trades are considered, a difference of only a few BA points can be worth hundreds of thousands of dollars.

Switch hitters are valuable players because they can adjust to different types of pitchers. Facing a left-handed pitcher, a switch hitter would usually bat right-handed because the ball is more likely to move in toward the batter, making it easier to hit. Managers need to know a switch hitter's BA from each side of the plate when deciding whether to have that player face a left-handed or right-handed pitcher.

The switch-hitting statistics for Eddie Murray and Orlando Merced looked like those shown in Table 1.5.

**Table 1.5**

**1991 Left- and Right-Handed Batting Statistics**

|  | EDDIE MURRAY BATTING AVERAGE | ORLANDO MERCED BATTING AVERAGE |
|---|---|---|
| LEFT-HANDED | .295 | .285 |
| RIGHT-HANDED | .217 | .208 |
| TOTAL | .260 | .275 |

QUESTION:

**Provide a forecast of the number of replacement tires that will be demanded. (Remember, every passenger mile is driven on four tires.)**

## Problem 2: Replacement-Tire Forecast

The tire industry manufactures tires for a variety of vehicles and aircraft around the world. Demand forecasts for tires[15] are developed separately for different vehicle types, by geographic region, and by whether the tires are for "original equipment" (i.e., tires that are bundled in the sale of new vehicles) or "replacement."

We shall be concerned here with automobile passenger tires sold in North America in the replacement market. Tires on automobiles are replaced when they wear out or are damaged beyond repair. The annual demand for replacement tires depends, therefore, on their longevity (the number of miles driven before a tire wears out) and the total number of passenger miles driven per year.

---

[15] This problem is based on data in *Firestone Tire and Rubber Company* (see Chapter 4).

## Table 1.6

| PROJECTED LONGEVITY (MILES) | PERCENT OF TIRES |
|---|---|
| 18,000 | 20% |
| 24,000 | 20% |
| 32,000 | 20% |
| 42,000 | 20% |
| 80,000 | 20% |

**QUESTION:**

**Interpret the data in the table. Do they support or refute the proposition that the rich got richer, the poor got poorer, and the middle class stagnated?**

Forecasts of the latter can be made with considerable accuracy, but tire longevity varies considerably, depending on road conditions encountered, driving style, condition of the vehicle, and type of tire. Data on tire longevity can be acquired by measuring treadwear on original-equipment tires, observing the mileage odometer, and making projections based on knowledge of the rate at which treadwear increases with mileage.

Recently, a study of treadwear on 50,000 vehicles projected longevity[16] as shown in Table 1.6. Passenger miles were forecast to be one trillion in the year in question.

### Problem 3: Did the Rich Get Richer?

In the spring of 1992, a debate among economists and demographers played a role in the presidential campaign. Did the "rich get richer and the poor get poorer" during the Reagan-Bush years? Bill Clinton said "yes," and he cited supporting data. President Bush and his supporters were quick with rebuttals.[17]

Two reports, "correcting" errors made by analysts who concluded that the income gap grew, were released in the summer of 1992, and both reports were widely praised and denounced—depending on one's political leanings.[18] One table, in particular, seemed to show that people who were relatively poor in 1977 did much better in the 1980s than people who started out relatively rich. This was precisely the opposite conclusion being preached by candidate Clinton (by then the Democratic nominee). In fact, one might even argue, based on this analysis, that "trickle down" economics actually worked.

The table in question (Table 1.7) is based on responses to a panel survey in which the same people (aged 25 to 54 in 1977) were followed from 1977 through 1986.

### Table 1.7

**Average Family Income and Change in Average Family Income, 1977–1986, of Families Grouped by Their Income Quintile in 1977[19] (1991 Dollars)**

| QUINTILE IN 1977 | AVERAGE FAMILY INCOME | | CHANGE IN AVERAGE FAMILY INCOME | |
|---|---|---|---|---|
| | 1977 | 1986 | AMOUNT | PERCENTAGE |
| First | $15,853 | $27,998 | $12,145 | 77% |
| Second | 31,340 | 43,041 | 11,701 | 37 |
| Third | 43,297 | 51,796 | 8,499 | 20 |
| Fourth | 57,486 | 63,314 | 5,828 | 10 |
| Fifth | 92,531 | 97,140 | 4,609 | 5 |

---

[16] The data are presented in just five categories for the sake of simplicity.

[17] As background on the debate, see Anne B. Fisher, "The New Debate Over the Very Rich," *Fortune,* June 29, 1992, pp. 42-54, and Marvin H. Kosters, "The Rise in Income Inequality," *The American Enterprise,* November/December, 1992, pp. 29-37.

[18] Isabel V. Sawhill & Mark Condon, "Is U.S. Income Inequality Really Growing? Sorting Out the Fairness Question," *Policy Bites,* The Urban Institute, June 1992; and "Household Income Changes Over Time: Some Basic Questions and Facts," U.S. Department of the Treasury, Office of Tax Analysis, July 1992.

[19] Derived from Isabel V. Sawhill & Mark Condon, *op. cit.* Reproduced with permission.

# WORKED EXAMPLES IN DATA ANALYSIS USING SPREADSHEETS

All spreadsheets permit you to produce charts and other analyses like those contained in this chapter. Because summarizing data in the form of charts, tables, or summary statistics gives you insight and lets you communicate your findings to others, this section explains a few tricks that make reasonably sophisticated summaries quite easy to produce. We illustrate those tricks using Excel 5.0. Other spreadsheets and other versions of Excel can do similar analyses, but you must learn different commands.

We assume that you have taken the Excel tutorials and have sufficient knowledge of Excel to perform basic functions without detailed instructions on keystrokes. Where appropriate, we give tips on how to perform certain operations using special tools built into Excel.

In this section, we show how to obtain summary statistics, make histogram and cumugram charts, compute fractiles and correlation coefficients, and produce various forms of scatter diagrams and time-series charts. We illustrate these techniques using two data files that are included in your data diskette: HTWT.XLS, which shows height, weight, and gender of each of 768 students in a recent first-year MBA class at Harvard Business School; and RETAIL.XLS, which shows retail sales and advertising in the United States by month from June 1982 through February 1988.

## Analysis of a Single Variable

***Summary Statistics.*** To start the analysis, open the file HTWT.XLS. (To avoid accidentally overwriting the data, start by saving the file as HTWT1.XLS.) Table 1.8 displays the first few rows of data (the actual data extend down to row 774).

**Table 1.8**_____

|   | A | B | C | D | E | F | G |
|---|---|---|---|---|---|---|---|
| 1 | **HTWT: Survey Response** | | | | | | |
| 2 | Height, Weight and Gender of a First Year MBA Class | | | | | | |
| 3 | | | | | | | |
| 4 | | | Height | Weight | 0=Male | | |
| 5 | | | (Inches) | (pounds) | 1=Female | | |
| 6 | | | **HT** | **WT** | **M/F** | | |
| 7 | | | 68 | 140 | 0 | | |
| 8 | | | 69 | 155 | 0 | | |
| 9 | | | 66 | 120 | 0 | | |
| 10 | | | 72 | 180 | 0 | | |
| 11 | | | 72 | 165 | 0 | | |
| 12 | | | 69 | 175 | 0 | | |
| 13 | | | 72 | 165 | 0 | | |
| 14 | | | 71 | 130 | 0 | | |
| 15 | | | 71 | 175 . | 0 | | |

Table 1.9 shows how to compute summary statistics for the height data that appear in column C in Table 1.8. The first column of Table 1.9 on the following page gives the name of the statistic, the second column gives the Excel function that computes the statistic, and the third column gives the value of the statistic.

Harvard Business School note 2-191-113. Worked Examples in Data Analysis Using Spreadsheets, was prepared by Professor Arthur Schleifer, Jr.

**Table 1.9**

| SUMMARY STATISTIC | EXCEL FUNCTION | VALUE OF STATISTIC |
|---|---|---|
| Number of Observations | =COUNT(C7:C774) | 768 |
| Smallest Value | =MIN(C7:C774) | 58 |
| Largest Value | =MAX(C7:C774) | 80 |
| Mean | =AVERAGE(C7:C774) | 69.5156 |
| Median* | =MEDIAN(C7:C774) | 70 |
| Mode | =MODE(C7:C774) | 72 |
| Standard Deviation** | =STDEVP(C7:C774) | 3.4422 |

*If there are an odd number of observations, Excel will give the value of the middle observation; if the number of observations is even, Excel will give the average of the two middle values. Thus it will give 5 as the median of 1, 2, 5, 17, 100, and 3.5 as the median of 1, 2, 2, 5, 17, 100. These results may differ from the results you get using a cumugram (see the discussion on fractiles later in this section). The differences will seldom be material, but in case of doubt, use the cumugram method.

**The function =STDEVP gives the population standard deviation, the value that corresponds to the standard deviation as defined in this chapter. The function =STDEV gives the sample standard deviation, a statistic that need not concern us now, but one that we shall find useful in later chapters.

***Histograms.***    To create a histogram, (1) define "bins" into which the individual observations can be sorted, then (2) use Excel's Histogram routine to count the frequency with which values fall into each bin and to plot the result.

For the height data, we have seen that the smallest value is 58 inches and the largest 80 inches. Therefore we can create bins as a column of integers starting at 58 and ending at 80.

For these exercises you will use the file named HTWT1.XLS, which you previously saved.

To create the bins:

- Type **Bin** in cell F6 and **Frequency** in cell G6.
- Type **58** in cell F7 and **59** in cell F8.
- Highlight cells F7 and F8, release the mouse button, then move the cursor to the lower right-hand corner (the "fill handle" of the cell containing 59). The cursor changes to a black plus sign (+).
- Drag the fill handle down until you reach 80 (row 29). If you fall short of this row, repeat from where you stopped. If you overshoot, delete the entries above 80. When you finish, the range F7:F29 should be highlighted.

Now, to perform the analysis and create the histogram:

- Click the **Tools** menu, then click **Data Analysis**.* A menu of analytic tools displays.
- Highlight **Histogram** and click **OK**. A Histogram dialog box displays.
- In the Histogram dialog box, type **C7:C774** in the box next to Input Range.
- Type **F7:F29** in the Bin Range section of the dialog box.

---

* If you don't see a Data Analysis option on the Tools menu, click Add-Ins, highlight Analysis ToolPak in the Add-Ins dialog box and click OK. Then click the Tools menu again. Now you should see a Data Analysis option.

▸ If you like, you may specify an Output Range that puts the histogram on the same worksheet as your original data. However, in most cases you will want to accept the default New Worksheet Ply, which puts the output into a separate worksheet.

▸ Make sure that the boxes for Pareto and Cumulative Percentage do not contain an x, and that the box for Chart Output is selected (contains an x). (Click on the box to add an x, or click again to remove an x you don't want.)

▸ When all the dialog box settings are correct, click **OK**.

Excel produces two columns in a new worksheet, as shown in Table 1.10. The first column contains the bin values and the second contains the number of observations in each bin. The number 2 in the Frequency column to the right of 58 in the Bin column means that there were two observations with values of 58 or more but lower than 59 (the next value in the Bin column). (In this sample, all values are integers, so you can interpret this as meaning that two heights were reported as 58 inches exactly. Had heights been reported to one-tenth of an inch, the Frequency column would give the number of observations for which reported heights were 58.0, 58.1, ... 58.9 inches, but not for 59.0 inches.) Notice that there is one height of exactly 80 inches, but no heights opposite "More" (meaning more than 80 inches) in the Bin column.

**Table 1.10**

| | A | B | C | D | E | F | G | H | I | |
|---|---|---|---|---|---|---|---|---|---|---|
| **1** | *Bin* | *Frequency* | | | | | | | | |
| **2** | 58 | 2 | | | | | | | | |
| **3** | 59 | 0 | | | | | | | | |
| **4** | 60 | 6 | | | | | | | | |
| **5** | 61 | 3 | | | | | | | | |
| **6** | 62 | 10 | | | | | | | | |
| **7** | 63 | 17 | | | | | | | | |
| **8** | 64 | 26 | | | | | | | | |
| **9** | 65 | 36 | | | | | | | | |
| **10** | 66 | 51 | | | | | | | | |
| **11** | 67 | 51 | | | | | | | | |
| **12** | 68 | 76 | | | | | | | | |
| **13** | 69 | 82 | | | | | | | | |
| **14** | 70 | 98 | | | | | | | | |
| **15** | 71 | 60 | | | | | | | | |
| **16** | 72 | 105 | | | | | | | | |
| **17** | 73 | 57 | | | | | | | | |
| **18** | 74 | 50 | | | | | | | | |
| **19** | 75 | 21 | | | | | | | | |
| **20** | 76 | 9 | | | | | | | | |
| **21** | 77 | 3 | | | | | | | | |
| **22** | 78 | 2 | | | | | | | | |
| **23** | 79 | 2 | | | | | | | | |
| **24** | 80 | 1 | | | | | | | | |
| **25** | More | 0 | | | | | | | | |
| **26** | | | | | | | | | | |

Next to the two columns of numbers, Excel produces a histogram chart, as shown in Figure 1.23. Notice that the bars are labeled with the bin value. In this case, the labeling conveys exactly the right information: there were 51 heights of 66 inches, for example, as the chart reports.

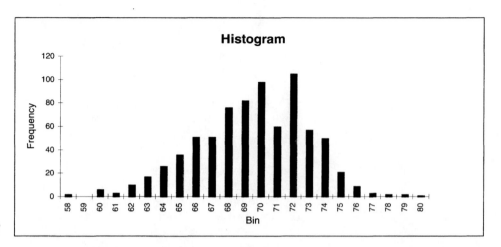

***Figure 1.23***

Let's plot the data again using bin values increasing by two—58, 60, 62 ..., 80. Copy the height, weight, and gender data to a new worksheet, using the Copy and Paste commands, create the bins and then the histogram, as in Figure 1.24.

The label for the first bar, 58, represents the number of heights that were either 58 or 59 inches; similarly, the label 70 represents the number that were either 70 or 71, etc. You have to be careful when you read histograms produced by Excel.

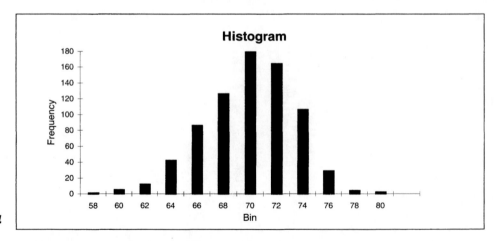

***Figure 1.24***

***Histogram of Relative Frequencies.*** Taking the results in Figure 1.24, suppose we wanted the vertical axis to represent *relative* frequencies, i.e., the fraction of observations that fell into each bin. For instance, 180 observations fell into the 70 bin, representing the number of students with heights of 70 or 71 inches. This is a fraction (180/768 = 0.234, or 23.4%) of all students. Let's construct a graph to show frequencies in terms of such fractions.

Start with the two-column output generated by the second histogram example (see Table 1.11). At the bottom of the Frequency column (cell B15), have Excel compute the total number of observations (we know that the total is 768, but suppose we didn't).

**Table 1.11** _____

|    | A    | B         | C | D | E | F | G | H | I |   |
|----|------|-----------|---|---|---|---|---|---|---|---|
| 1  | Bin  | Frequency |   |   |   |   |   |   |   |   |
| 2  | 58   | 2         |   |   |   |   |   |   |   |   |
| 3  | 60   | 6         |   |   |   |   |   |   |   |   |
| 4  | 62   | 13        |   |   |   |   |   |   |   |   |
| 5  | 64   | 43        |   |   |   |   |   |   |   |   |
| 6  | 66   | 87        |   |   |   |   |   |   |   |   |
| 7  | 68   | 127       |   |   |   |   |   |   |   |   |
| 8  | 70   | 180       |   |   |   |   |   |   |   |   |
| 9  | 72   | 165       |   |   |   |   |   |   |   |   |
| 10 | 74   | 107       |   |   |   |   |   |   |   |   |
| 11 | 76   | 30        |   |   |   |   |   |   |   |   |
| 12 | 78   | 5         |   |   |   |   |   |   |   |   |
| 13 | 80   | 3         |   |   |   |   |   |   |   |   |
| 14 | More | 0         |   |   |   |   |   |   |   |   |
| 15 |      |           |   |   |   |   |   |   |   |   |

*TIP:*

You can type = , then simply put the cursor on cell B2, type /, then place the cursor on cell B15 and press the F4 key to add $. Because you want to divide each value in the B column by 768 (the value in B15), you want Excel to recognize B15 as an "absolute" address. The format $B$15 signifies an absolute address.

To sum the column:

▸ Click cell **B15**, click the **AutoSum** ($\Sigma$) **button** on the toolbar, then press [**Enter**].

▸ In cell C2, type the formula **=B2/$B$15** and press [**Enter**].

▸ Now drag the fill handle in cell C2 down through cell C15. The results are shown in Table 1.12.

**Table 1.12** _____

|    | A    | B         | C        | D | E | F | G | H | I |   |
|----|------|-----------|----------|---|---|---|---|---|---|---|
| 1  | Bin  | Frequency | Rel Freq |   |   |   |   |   |   |   |
| 2  | 58   | 2         | 0.002604 |   |   |   |   |   |   |   |
| 3  | 60   | 6         | 0.007813 |   |   |   |   |   |   |   |
| 4  | 62   | 13        | 0.016927 |   |   |   |   |   |   |   |
| 5  | 64   | 43        | 0.05599  |   |   |   |   |   |   |   |
| 6  | 66   | 87        | 0.113281 |   |   |   |   |   |   |   |
| 7  | 68   | 127       | 0.165365 |   |   |   |   |   |   |   |
| 8  | 70   | 180       | 0.234375 |   |   |   |   |   |   |   |
| 9  | 72   | 165       | 0.214844 |   |   |   |   |   |   |   |
| 10 | 74   | 107       | 0.139323 |   |   |   |   |   |   |   |
| 11 | 76   | 30        | 0.039063 |   |   |   |   |   |   |   |
| 12 | 78   | 5         | 0.00651  |   |   |   |   |   |   |   |
| 13 | 80   | 3         | 0.003906 |   |   |   |   |   |   |   |
| 14 | More | 0         | 0        |   |   |   |   |   |   |   |
| 15 |      | 768       | 1        |   |   |   |   |   |   |   |

You can use Excel's ChartWizard to draw the histogram of relative frequencies. To begin, highlight the Bin column and the Relative Frequency column:

▸ Hold down [**Ctrl**] (if you're using Windows) or [**Command**] (on the Macintosh), click in cell **A2**, and drag from A2 to A13.

▸ Release the mouse button (but continue to hold down [Ctrl] or [Command]), click in cell **C2**, and drag from C2 to C13.

▶ Click the **ChartWizard icon** on the toolbar. The cursor becomes a plus sign (+) with a bar chart at the lower right.

▶ Click and drag the cursor on your worksheet to form a rectangle (if you prefer, you can use a new worksheet).

Now the ChartWizard takes over.

▶ It asks whether the range you have selected ($A$2:$A$13,$C$2:$C$13) is correct. Since it is correct, click **Next**.

▶ Now it asks you to select a chart type. Double-click **Column**.

▶ Select a chart format by double-clicking on "**1**."

▶ In the Control box that appears, specify that the data are in Columns, that you are using the first 1 column for category (X) axis labels, and that you are using the first 0 rows for legend text. Then click **Next**.

▶ ChartWizard then invites you to provide various titles. We do not need a legend, so click **No** under Add a Legend? You may, at your option, add chart and axis titles. Click **Finish** to tell the ChartWizard to create the chart. After it appears, you can use the resize arrow at the lower-right corner of the chart to change its width and height until it looks something like Figure 1.25.

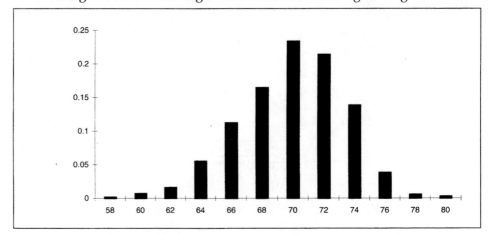

**Figure 1.25**

***Cumugrams.***   Excel has various routines for drawing cumulative distributions, but none of them produces a stairstep cumugram that correctly displays the fraction of observations that lie at or below any specified value.

A cumugram add-in (CUMUGRAM.XLA) is provided on your data diskette. Copy it to a directory or folder. When you want to use it:

▶ Open the file that contains the add-in, click the **Window** menu, and switch back to your original workbook.

▶ Highlight the column of data that contains the variable whose cumugram you want, and simultaneously press [**Ctrl**] (if you're in Windows) or [**Command**] (on the Macintosh), [**Shift**], and [**C**]. A cumugram chart appears on a worksheet called Cumugram. See Figure 1.26 for a cumugram of the height variable.

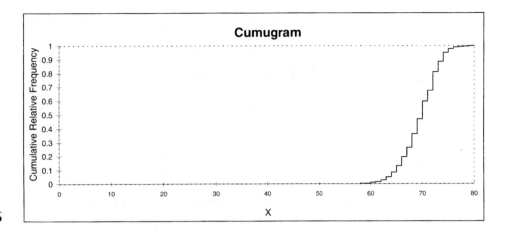

**Figure 1.26**

**TIP:**

The cumugram add-in doesn't always do a good job of setting the horizontal scale values. You can get rid of all the white space to the left of the cumugram by changing the scale. To do so, double-click the horizontal axis. When a Format Axis menu pops up, choose the Scale tab, then change the minimum value to 55 and the maximum value to 85. Click OK to get a cumugram like that shown in Figure 1.27.

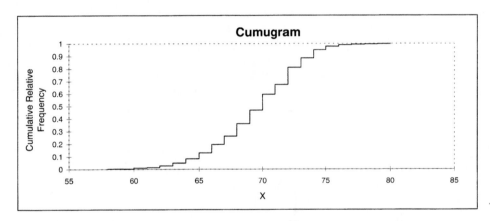

**Figure 1.27**

***Fractiles.***   Excel has various routines that are supposed to give fractile-like results, but they do not conform to the standard (and economically useful) definition of a fractile. The easiest way to get a fractile is by way of the cumugram. Figure 1.28, which has a more detailed scale, shows that the three quartiles (the 0.25, 0.50, and 0.75 fractiles) are respectively 67, 70, and 72 for the height data.

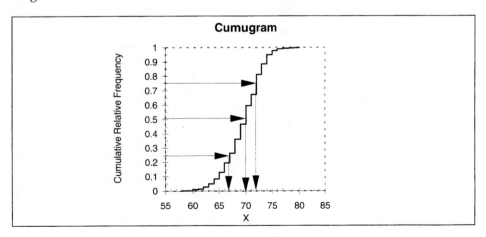

**Figure 1.28**

## Analysis of Two Variables

Open the HTWT1.XLS data file again, and move the data to another worksheet in the same location. You'll use this file for your work on scatter diagrams.

***Scatter Diagrams.***    You can use Excel's ChartWizard to plot a scatter diagram of height against weight. To start:

▶ Highlight the range **C7:D774** (the fastest way to do this is to highlight cells C7 and D7, then press **[Ctrl] [Shift]**), and the **[↓]** , then click the ChartWizard button. Finally, use the mouse to draw a rectangle on your spreadsheet. The ChartWizard takes over.

▶ Look at the Range text box, and verify that you have chosen C7:D774. Click **Next**.

▶ Choose **XY (Scatter)** for the chart type, and click **Next**.

▶ Choose chart format **1**, and click **Next**.

▶ In the control boxes to the right of the sample chart, indicate that the Data Series is in **Columns**, that the first **1** column is for category (X) data, and the first **0** row is for legend text. Click **Next** when you have checked your selections.

▶ Select **No** under Add a Legend? In the Chart Title text box, type **Scatter Diagram**, then type **Height** next to category (X) and **Weight** next to Value (Y) and click **Finish**. When your diagram appears on the spreadsheet, adjust its shape with the resize arrow until it looks something like the one shown in Figure 1.29.

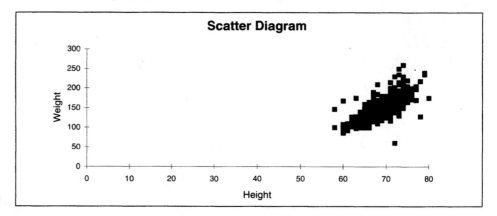

***Figure 1.29***

Now you may want to rescale the horizontal axis. To make this change:

▶ Double-click the chart to activate it, then double-click on the **horizontal scale markers**. A Format Axis dialog box displays. Click the **Scale** tab, then change the Minimum value to **55** and change the Major Unit to **5** to spread out the data points. Click **OK**.

▶ You could double-click the vertical scale and repeat the process if you wanted to expand the vertical scale.

To reformat the data points:

▶ Double-click the chart if you need to activate it, then click on any data point in the chart. A Format Data Series dialog box displays (you may have to click on several different data points to obtain the correct dialog box).

▶ In the dialog box, choose the **Patterns** tab, which offers you a choice of marker shapes as well as background and foreground colors. Try different combinations.

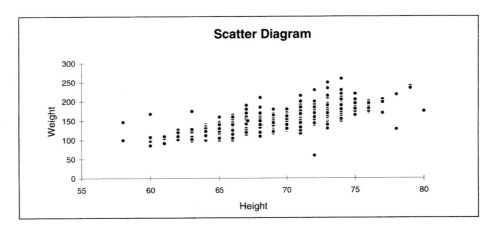

**Figure 1.30**

In the scatter diagram shown in Figure 1.30, the marker has been changed from a solid square to a circle with a white foreground and a black background.* To do that:

▪ On the Patterns tab, click the scroll arrow opposite Style to open the drop-down menu and click the circle.

▪ Click the scroll arrow opposite Foreground and choose the white square.

▪ Click the scroll arrow opposite Background, choose the black square, and click **OK**.

***Scatter Diagrams with Identifiers.*** Scatter diagrams with identifiers convey a great deal of information, but are difficult to produce. In this section, we show how to produce a diagram like Figure 1.6 of this chapter, which shows height vs. weight, with different markers for men and women.

Start by copying the three columns in HTWT.XLS (height, weight, and gender) to a new worksheet in the same location. Then sort the data so that all the men (Gender = 0) appear first, followed by all the women. To do that:

▪ Highlight the range **C7:E774** and click **Data**, then click **Sort**. The Sort dialog box opens.

▪ In the dialog box, click the scroll arrow in the Sort By box and select M/F. The Ascending option should be selected. Click **OK**.

Now :

▪ Move the height column (C4:C774) to **B4:B774**. (Adjust column width if necessary.)

▪ Move the weight data for men (D4:D603) to **C4:C603**.

You now have one column of height data and two columns of weight data: column C has 171 blank rows at the bottom, and column D has 597 blank rows at the top. Save your work so far.

Highlight the range B7:D774, click the **ChartWizard** button, and drag a rectangle on the spreadsheet. To plot the scatter diagram with the ChartWizard:

▪ Look at the Range text box, and verify that you have chosen B7:D774. Click **Next**.

▪ Choose **XY (Scatter)** for the chart type, then click **Next**.

---

* This may be easier to see on-screen if you choose bright colors such as reds, blues, greens, etc.

> ● Choose chart format **1**, then click **Next**.

> ● In the control boxes to the right of the chart, select **Data Series** in Columns, first 1 column for category (X) data and **first 0 row** for legend text.

> ● For the Chart Title, type **Scatter Diagram with Identifier**, with Height for Category (X) and Weight for Value (Y).

After rescaling the axes and changing markers, you will obtain a chart like Figure 1.31, where Series 1 represents men and Series 2 represents women.

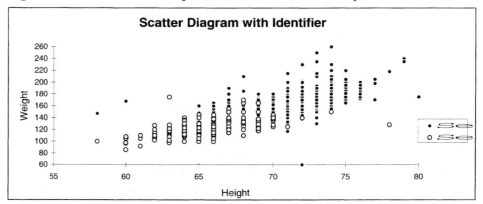

*Figure 1.31*

***Correlation.*** You can obtain the correlation coefficient using Excel's Correl function. To obtain the correlation between height and weight, click any empty cell on the worksheet and type: **=Correl(C7:C774,D7:D774)**, then press [**Enter**].

You will get a correlation coefficient of 0.745255.

## Time Series

Finally, we show how to obtain the simple time series of Retail Sales shown in Figure 1.7 of this chapter, as well as the stack graph showing sales one year at a time (Figure 1.8).

Open RETAIL.XLS and save it as RETAIL1.XLS. Highlight cells **C9:D77** (the column of Dates and the column of Actual Retail Sales). Click the ChartWizard and draw a rectangle with the mouse. This time, choose Line as the chart type (sales corresponding to successive months are plotted at equally spaced intervals in a Line chart) and choose 2 as the format. After following the procedures described in the ChartWizard, then rescaling the axes, you should obtain a chart that looks something like Figure 1.32.

*Figure 1.32*

To create the stacked graph:

▶ First find an empty grid 13 rows high by 8 columns wide (start at cell H6, for example). In cell H7, type **Jan**, then drag the fill handle down the column, which will automatically fill in three-letter abbreviations for the other months. Don't go too far; the yearly cycle will repeat if you drag further than 12 months.

▶ In cell I6, type **1982** and in J6 type **1983.** Highlight these two cells and then drag the fill handle to the right, to cell O6.

▶ Now copy the column of actual sales (D9:D77) to column I, starting with row 12 opposite Jun, since the data series starts with June 1982. Then copy the actual sales data starting in January 1983 (cell I19) into Column J, row 7 (opposite Jan) and so forth (you may need to widen the columns to make the data fit). When you finish, save your work; the grid should look like Table 1.13.

▶ Next, highlight the grid you have just created, invoke the ChartWizard, specify Line as the chart type and 1 as the format. In Step 4 of the ChartWizard procedure, indicate that the Data Series is in Columns, that the first **1** column will be used for category (X) axis labels, and that the first **1** row will be used for legend text. After scaling the axes, you should obtain a chart that looks something like Figure 1.33.

**Table 1.13**

|   | H | I | J | K | L | M | N | O |   |
|---|---|---|---|---|---|---|---|---|---|
| 6 |   | 1982 | 1983 | 1984 | 1985 | 1986 | 1987 | 1988 |   |
| 7 | Jan |   | 81.34 | 93.09 | 98.82 | 105.64 | 106.39 | 113.64 |   |
| 8 | Feb |   | 78.88 | 93.69 | 95.59 | 99.66 | 105.80 | 115.10 |   |
| 9 | Mar |   | 93.76 | 104.29 | 110.17 | 114.24 | 120.44 |   |   |
| 10 | Apr |   | 93.97 | 104.34 | 113.11 | 115.13 | 124.74 |   |   |
| 11 | May |   | 97.84 | 111.31 | 120.19 | 126.09 | 128.69 |   |   |
| 12 | Jun | 88.97 | 100.61 | 111.98 | 114.78 | 120.98 | 128.99 |   |   |
| 13 | Jul | 91.21 | 99.56 | 106.88 | 115.23 | 121.47 | 129.26 |   |   |
| 14 | Aug | 89.64 | 100.23 | 111.16 | 120.77 | 124.72 | 131.54 |   |   |
| 15 | Sep | 88.16 | 97.97 | 104.03 | 113.84 | 125.44 | 124.52 |   |   |
| 16 | Oct | 91.42 | 100.67 | 109.55 | 115.75 | 123.84 | 128.30 |   |   |
| 17 | Nov | 94.20 | 103.87 | 113.54 | 118.06 | 121.37 | 126.90 |   |   |
| 18 | Dec | 113.19 | 125.76 | 132.26 | 138.65 | 152.11 | 157.19 |   |   |

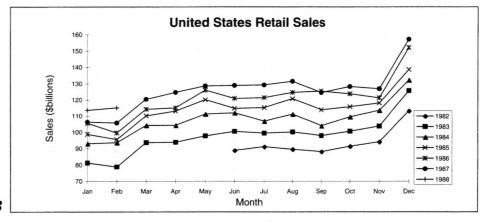

**Figure 1.33**

# 2 ▼ SAMPLING AND STATISTICAL INFERENCE

## INTRODUCTION

This chapter describes what you can infer about a population from a sample of observations drawn from that population. It focuses on inferences about population means and percents.[1] Examples of population means include the average annual per capita purchases by a population of customers, and average waiting time for customers trying to contact an airline reservation system. An example of a population percent is the percent of the United States workforce that is unemployed.[2]

The key concept of statistical inference is that although a sample provides useful information about a population mean or percent, that information is imperfect. We are left with some uncertainty about its true value. Statistical inference provides ways of estimating the true value and of quantifying our uncertainty about that estimate.

**Samples** are taken when it is impossible, impractical, or too expensive to obtain complete data on a relevant population. For example, you ask a sample of people drawn from a target population how much each intends to spend on a product, and from their responses you make an inference about actual sales per capita for the whole target population. As another example, you take a sample of telephone calls coming into an airline reservation system, measure the amount of time (if any) each call is kept waiting, and from this make an inference about the average waiting time for all calls.

This chapter gives you a conceptual overview of issues in sampling and inference. Some of the basic ideas are subtle. The best way to test your understanding of these ideas is to work through the examples and the exercises. When you get a numerical result, ask yourself what that result means. The formulas that are important in sampling are quite simple; they are collected together in the Appendix to this chapter so that you can readily access them.

Harvard Business School note 9-191-092. This note was prepared by Professor Arthur Schleifer, Jr. Copyright © 1993 by the President and Fellows of Harvard College.

---

[1] Sometimes we are interested in population totals rather than in means or percents. For example, we might be more interested in total purchases made by a population of customers than in average per capita purchases. Whatever we know about a population mean or percent can readily be translated into knowledge about a population total by multiplying the mean or percent by the size of the population.

[2] Inferences can also be made about processes. For example, we might want to make inferences about the long-run average rate of defects of a production process. Everything we say about populations is applicable to processes as well, but we shall focus our discussion on populations only.

For those of you who have previously studied sampling theory, it is important to understand that there are different levels of refinement in approaching the subject. You may have learned more accurate or more powerful methods than those presented here. These come at a cost of increasing complexity. In many managerial situations, it is not critical to know that a 95% confidence interval really extends from 200 to 250, when a rough-and-ready calculation might indicate that it extends from 190 to 260; either result will often lead to the same conclusion. In situations where very precise results are critical, you should seek expert advice.

Almost all the concepts discussed in this chapter come up again in the context of regression. Some of the concepts included here (for instance, the *t*-statistic or degrees of freedom) are not crucial for your understanding of sampling and inference, but introduce topics that are important in regression. This and subsequent chapters on regression should make you aware of the close linkages among sampling, inference, and regression, and give you two contexts in which these concepts play an important role.

# SAMPLING ERROR

A sample may fail to tell you the exact value of a population mean or percent[3] due to sampling error. Sampling error arises from the fact that the sample mean may differ from its counterpart in the population due to the "luck of the draw." It is one of several sources of error in making inferences about a population from a sample.

## ▼ Inferences from a Sample

Even if a sample is "representative"[4] of the population from which it is drawn, it provides only imperfect information about that population, owing in part to sampling error. As an illustration, suppose you ask 100 potential customers how much they will spend on a proposed new product next year. The first says $10, the second $92, the third "nothing," and so on. You add up the 100 responses, divide by 100, and obtain $32.51 as your **sample average**. At this point, you want to make an inference from these responses about how much will be spent by the average potential customer in your entire market (the target population) next year. You could make the following inferences:

a)   "My best estimate of average sales per potential customer is $32.51."

b)   "Average sales per potential customer will be between $27.37 and $37.65 with 95% confidence."

c)   "Average sales per potential customer will be greater than the breakeven amount of $27 at a 2½% level of significance."

An inference like (a) is called **statistical estimation**, (b) is a **confidence interval**, and (c) is a **test of** (statistical) **significance**.

---

[3] For most of this section we shall discuss population means only; at the end, we shall introduce the very minor modifications that apply for population percents.

[4] The only way to assure that the sample is representative is via some form of random sampling. We discuss this concept more fully later in this chapter.

## Estimation and Confidence Intervals

**Statistical estimation** is a relatively straightforward procedure: when the distribution of values in the population is fairly symmetric and there are no extreme outliers, the **sample mean** ($m$) serves as a good estimate of the population mean. In the sales per customer example, $32.51 serves as a good estimate of the population mean.

   **Confidence intervals**, on the other hand, are somewhat more subtle. Confidence in how close a sample estimate is to the true population mean depends on the **sample size** ($n$), and on the dispersion of the sample observations, as measured by the **sample standard deviation** ($s$).[5] Everything else being equal, your uncertainty about the value of a population mean will decrease as the sample size increases and the dispersion in the sample values decreases. To illustrate, in the example above, you would feel more confident that the population mean is close to $32.51 if your sample mean of $32.51 came from a sample of 400 respondents, instead of only 100. Similarly, you would feel more confident that the population mean is close to the sample mean if each of your 100 respondents expected to spend between $32 and $33 on the product next year, and less confident if their responses ranged from "nothing" to $500.

   The level of confidence about the value of a population mean can be expressed in terms of a **confidence distribution.** In making inferences about a population mean, the mean of the confidence distribution is equal to the sample mean $m$, and its standard deviation (called the **standard error**) is equal to the sample standard deviation $s$ divided by the square root of the sample size, $n$:

$$\text{standard error} = s/\sqrt{n}$$

The standard error decreases as the dispersion in the sample decreases and as the sample size increases.

   The shape of a confidence distribution is essentially normal or bell-shaped, regardless of the shape of the distribution of values within the population itself. As is the case for *any* normal distribution, a value within one standard deviation above or below the mean occurs with 68% confidence; a value within two standard deviations above or below the mean has 95% confidence; and a value within three standard deviations has 99.7% confidence. Figure 2.1 portrays these relationships for a confidence distribution.

   From the confidence distribution, you can construct a confidence interval for the population mean. A confidence interval states both a range within which the true value of the population mean may lie, as well as a level of confidence that the population mean does, in fact, lie within that interval. Confidence intervals of different lengths, and correspondingly different levels of confidence, can be constructed from a given sample. In general, we would prefer confidence intervals to be narrow rather than wide, since narrow intervals imply greater certainty about the population mean, and we would like the confidence level to be as high as possible. Unfortunately, for a sample that has already been taken, these preferences constitute a tradeoff: the narrower the confidence interval, the lower the confidence that the true value of the population mean lies within the interval. Conversely, the higher you want your confidence to be that the population mean lies within a given interval, the wider the interval must be. The only way you can achieve both objectives—to have a narrow interval with high confidence—is to take a large sample.

---

[5] See the opening section of the Appendix to this chapter for a discussion of the sample standard deviation.

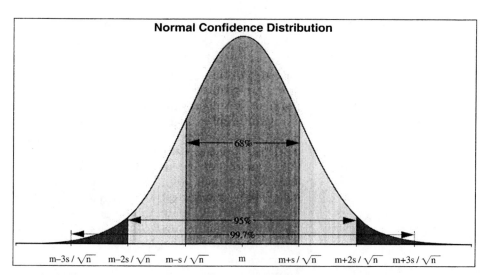

**Figure 2.1**

From the confidence distribution, you can construct a confidence interval for the population mean. A confidence interval is based entirely on three characteristics of a sample: the sample size, *n*; the sample mean, *m*; and the sample standard deviation, *s*. The population size is irrelevant. A confidence interval based on a sample with given values of *n*, *m*, and *s* will be the same, whether the sample in question is drawn from a population of 1,000 or a population of 1,000,000. It is a very common error for people to believe that an adequate sample should be some fixed percentage of the population, say 10%. Quite the contrary. It is the absolute size of the sample that determines accuracy.[6]

The following example illustrates how a confidence interval is constructed. A market researcher asks a sample of 100 potential customers how much they plan to spend on a product next year. The mean of this sample turns out to be $32.51 and the standard deviation is 25.7. The best estimate of what the average potential customer will spend is, therefore, $32.51. The standard error is $25.7/\sqrt{100} = 25.7/10 = 2.57$. Thus, with 68% confidence,[7] we can say that the average potential customer will spend between $32.51 − $2.57 and $32.51 + $2.57 (or between $29.94 and $35.08). Similarly, with 95% confidence, average expenditure will be between $27.37 and $37.65, and with 99.7% confidence, it will be between $24.80 and $40.22.

## Statistical Significance

A third type of inference you can make from a sample is a **test of significance**. Rather than estimating a point at which, or an interval within which, the population mean lies, you can indicate if the population mean is likely to fall above or below a critical value of interest, called *c*. For example, you may want to know whether average sales per capita is likely to exceed a breakeven level of $27. If the sample mean is $32.51 and thus lies above the critical value of $27, how likely is it that the population mean is on the same side of the critical value?

---

[6] For a slight qualification of this statement, see the section called Finite–Population Correction in the Appendix to this chapter.

[7] The 68% confidence can be interpreted as follows: if you sampled many different populations and constructed a 68% confidence interval for each sample, then 68% of the time the true population mean would lie within the corresponding interval.

To answer this question, you can first construct a confidence interval and then determine whether the interval overlaps the critical value. If it does not, the sample outcome is said to be **statistically significant**. If it does overlap the critical value, the sample outcome is said to be **not significant**. These tests have a corresponding **level of significance**, and the two should be reported together. A sample result is statistically significant at a level of 2½% when a critical value falls outside a 95% confidence interval and therefore lies in a region in which we have only 2½% confidence[8] that the population mean lies. Similarly, a test is statistically significant at a level of 0.15% when a critical value falls outside a 99.7% confidence interval.[9]

The case of launching a new product serves to illustrate tests and levels of significance. Suppose $n = 100$, $m = 32.51$, and $s = 25.7$. Then, as we saw before, a 95% confidence interval extends from 27.37 to 37.65, and does not cover the critical value of $c = 27$. Therefore, relative to 27, the sample outcome of 32.51 is statistically significant at the 2½% level.

***The t–statistic.*** Rather than determining statistical significance by constructing a confidence interval, the following shortcut procedure produces the same results. If $c$ represents the critical value, compute the statistic

$$t = (m - c)/\text{standard error} = (m - c)/(s/\sqrt{n}) \ .$$

Then if $t > 2$ or $t < -2$, the sample outcome is significant at the 2½% level. (Try the computation on the two examples above, and convince yourself that it yields the same results.) If $t > 3$ or $t < -3$, the sample outcome is significant at the 0.15% level.

***Significance vs. Importance.*** It is very important to realize that a result can be statistically significant but unimportant, or vice versa. Because it is extremely unlikely that the population mean or percent will be precisely equal to the critical value, a sufficiently large sample usually shows statistical significance, whereas smaller samples may not. For this reason, a statistically significant outcome may not be economically better than an outcome that is not statistically significant. For example, suppose a manager is trying to decide which of two new products, A or B, to introduce. Breakeven sales per capita are $27 for both A and B. The manager obtains a sample of 10,000 potential customers for product A, but only 100 for product B. The sample results are in Table 2.1.

**Table 2.1**

|  | PRODUCT A | PRODUCT B |
|---|---|---|
| $n$ | 10,000 | 100 |
| $m$ | 27.3 | 46.0 |
| $s$ | 10 | 100 |

---

[8] We have a 95% level of confidence that the population mean lies within the interval, and hence a 5% level of confidence that it lies outside. By virtue of the symmetry of the confidence distribution, we have just a 2½% level of confidence that the population mean lies below the lower limit of the confidence interval.

[9] These are examples of one-sided tests of significance. In the statistical literature, some tests are two-sided (essentially doubling the level of significance), but such tests are mentioned only for completeness, and need not concern us here.

For product A, a 95% confidence interval extends from 27.1 to 27.5, a result that is statistically significant relative to $c = 27$ at the 2½% level. For product B, a 95% confidence interval extends from 26 to 66, and hence the result is not significant at the 2½% level. If the manager must now decide which product to introduce, and can acquire no more data, what should she do?

Product A has higher prospects of breaking even, but not much potential for large profit. Product B has lower prospects of breaking even (more downside risk) but much more upside potential. Unless the manager were very risk-averse, she should prefer B to A.

## ▼ Sample Size

Taking a sample to obtain information about a population mean requires a decision about the sample size. How large a sample should you take? Since sampling is usually expensive, and the cost of sampling often increases with sample size, there is a tradeoff between more precision at higher cost and less precision at lower cost. To determine the appropriate sample size, you can first specify the length of a confidence interval and an associated confidence level that you would consider satisfactory, and then compute a sample size that will deliver such a confidence level and interval.

Suppose, for example, you want to say with 95% confidence that average annual expenditure for a target population is within an interval of length $L$. That is, if the sample mean turns out to be $32.51, you would like the sample size to be such that with 95% confidence you would know the population mean is between 32.51–0.5$L$ and 32.51 + 0.5$L$. How large a sample must you take to achieve this level of precision? If we knew the sample standard deviation, $s$, the answer would be simple. You would like the interval from $m - 2s/\sqrt{n}$ to $m + 2s/\sqrt{n}$ to have length $L$. That means that $4s/\sqrt{n} = L$, or $\sqrt{n} = 4s/L$, or $n = 16s^2/L^2$. If $s = 25.7$ and $L = 2$, then the required sample size would be $n = 2,642$. (By similar logic, the sample size for a 68% confidence interval is $n = 4s^2/L^2$, and for a 99.7% interval is $n = 36s^2/L^2$.)

A sample of this size might be prohibitively expensive. If you were willing to double the length of the interval $L$ from 2 to 4, you could reduce the size of the sample by a factor of *four*, from 2,642 to 661. That is because the length of the interval depends on $1/\sqrt{n}$ : if you quadruple $n$, you halve the length; if you reduce $n$ by a factor of 4, you double the length. In general, the process of choosing a sample size is an iterative one, in which you compare the tradeoffs between precision and cost.

The analysis above assumes that you know the value of the sample standard deviation $s$ before the sample is even drawn. Unfortunately, $s$ is a statistic whose value is computed *after* the sample is drawn. The only thing you can do to escape this logical trap is to *guess*[10] the value of $s$, and hope that your results are not too sensitive to a substantial misestimate.

## ▼ Confidence vs. Probability

When reporting that a 95% confidence interval for a population mean extends from $27.37 to $37.65, it is tempting to slip into the language of probability, and say that there is only a 5% probability that the true value of the population mean is outside this interval. Similarly, if the sample mean is $32.51, then, by virtue of the symmetry of the confidence distribution and the fact that its mean is equal to the sample mean, it is tempting to say that there is a 50-50 chance that the true population mean is greater than $32.51.

---

[10] Sometimes you can get a fair estimate of $s$ from a small pilot sample.

Such probabilistic interpretations are much more natural and appealing than the rather convoluted interpretation given in footnote 7. But are they legitimate?

Suppose, as before, a sample of 100 potential customers reveals how much each will spend on your product next year. In the past several years, average expenditure per customer has ranged from $10 to $15, and no product or competitive changes are likely to support a jump to the $27 – $38 range. For this reason, you must conclude that the 95% confidence interval extending from roughly $27 to $38 overstates the probability that demand per customer will fall in that range. You can only conclude that the luck of the draw led to a sample mean of $32.51 that, in this case, was too high.

If, on the other hand, you have no additional information to suggest that this sample result is substantially more or less likely than other possible results, then you can interpret the confidence distribution derived from the sample as a probability distribution, and you can treat a significance level as the probability that the population mean falls above or below a critical value.

## ▼ Population Percents

As indicated previously, almost everything that we have said regarding inferences for population means applies to population percents. Although it is natural to think in terms of percents (the percent of voters who will vote for candidate X; the percent of people who will buy our product, etc.), it is important for computational purposes to express percents in fractional form, e.g., 20% = 0.20. To emphasize this, we will use the language of fractions and not percents in this section.

When we are dealing with fractions, individual values can be coded as $0$s and $1$s. A person who will vote for candidate $X$ will be coded 1; a person voting for a different candidate will be coded 0, etc. The mean of this dummy variable is then the fraction of $1$s. Suppose we take a sample of $n$ observations, and that a fraction $f$ of those observations are $1$s. Then the sample fraction $f$ is the sample mean. Accordingly:

▶ The sample fraction $f$ is an estimate of the population fraction.

▶ A confidence distribution for the population fraction is normal with mean $f$ and standard error $s/\sqrt{n}$ .

▶ The 68%, 95%, and 99.7% confidence intervals are defined exactly as before, as are $t$ values.

While the value of $s$ can be computed for a dummy variable in exactly the same way as for any other variable, there is a shortcut formula available. For a dummy variable,

$$s = \sqrt{f*(1-f)*n/(n-1)} \quad ;$$

unless $n$ is quite small (10 or less), the term $n/(n-1)$ is close enough to 1 so that it can be safely ignored. Thus, to a very reasonable approximation,

$$s = \sqrt{f*(1-f)} .$$

***Example.*** A sample of 100 voters was asked for which of two candidates, X or Y, they would vote. Fifty-two said they would vote for X. Then $f = 0.52$, $s = \sqrt{0.52*(1-0.52)} = 0.4996$, and the standard error is $0.4996/\sqrt{100} = 0.04996$. A 95% confidence interval would extend from $0.52 - 2*0.04996 = 0.4201$ to $0.52 + 2*0.04996 = 0.6199$. The sample outcome is not significant at the 2½% level relative to a critical value of $c = 0.50$. (Had the sample size been 10,000, with 5,200 in favor of X, the sample outcome would have been statistically significant, as you should verify.)

Figure 2.2 shows how the standard deviation $s$ for a dummy variable depends on the sample fraction $f$. If you are quite sure, before you take a sample, that the sample fraction will not be less than 0.2 nor greater than 0.8, you can be equally sure that $s$ will be between 0.4 and 0.5.

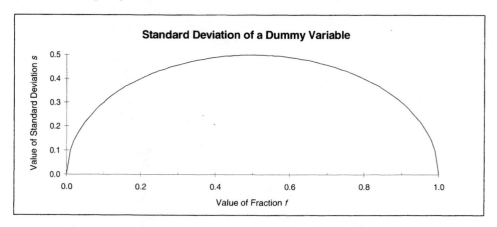

**Figure 2.2**

This is very helpful in sample–size problems. To illustrate, suppose you are conducting a national poll to determine the percent of voters who will vote for the Republican candidate in the next presidential election. Suppose that you want to state with 95% confidence that your results are within an interval of $L = 5$ percentage points. We can be quite sure that $f$ will be between 0.2 and 0.8, and hence that $s$ will be between 0.4 and 0.5. Let's assume the worst case—that $s = 0.5$. Then our sample size $n$ should be such that

$$n = 16s^2/L^2 = 16*0.5^2/0.05^2 = 1{,}600 \quad .$$

In fact, many national polls involve around 1,600 respondents, and are commonly reported as having a margin of error of 2½% (half the length of the confidence interval); the confidence level of 95% is implicit.

# SAMPLING IN THE REAL WORLD

Apart from random sampling error, there are two other sources of error in making inferences about a population from a sample. The first involves response bias and the second concerns the representativeness of the sample.

## Response Bias

Almost all questions about people's opinions, attitudes, expectations, or preferences involve response biases of various kinds. When 44% of the voters sampled in a public-opinion poll in June say they will vote for the Republican presidential candidate, and when the actual vote in November turns out to be 53% for the Republican, the polls are often said to have been "wrong." However, the discrepancy between 44% and 53% can seldom be accounted for by sampling error. Instead, it is mostly due to the fact that respondents did not do in November what they said they would do in June.

Such response bias stems from a number of factors. First, opinions change over time. Second, people do not always say what they will do or have done. Third, people cannot answer certain questions realistically; for example, they seldom know how much they will spend on a new product in the coming year. Fourth, the way in which a question is asked sometimes influences the response.

For example, of 764 people who were asked whether they agreed or disagreed with the statement "Advertising often persuades people to buy things they shouldn't buy," 76% agreed, 20% disagreed, and 4% had no opinion, while of 772 people who were asked a similar question about the statement "Advertising seldom persuades people to buy things they shouldn't buy," 40% agreed, 56% disagreed, and 4% had no opinion.[11]

Although the way a question is asked may influence the answer, asking the same question repeatedly can reveal changes in respondents' attitudes over time. The president's "report card" is generated by asking respondents periodically to assess the president's performance. As long as the question remains the same, a sharp drop in performance rating (if it cannot be explained as mere sampling error) is a good indication that the population at large has become less satisfied with performance. But a sharp drop that coincides with a rewording of the question may be nothing more than an indication of response bias.

## Representativeness

A sample should be representative of the population from which it is drawn. The easiest way to ensure representativeness is to take a sample in which every member of the target population has an equal chance of being included. Such a sample is called a **random sample**. To obtain a truly random sample, you must have a complete list of every member of the target population and you must select members from the list by a process that gives each member the same chance of being included in the sample. The random process may entail drawing names from a hat, using a table of random numbers, or telling a computer to select observations at random. If your target population is a group of people, collecting a sample entails one more step: you must track down the selected members and convince them to answer your questions. Obtaining a truly random sample is a time-consuming and difficult process. Often much more informal procedures—stopping people on the street, or in shopping malls, or in airports—are used.

Even when a serious attempt is made to obtain a random sample, the people who end up in the sample may not have been chosen in the prescribed manner for a variety of reasons. For example, in the United States, target populations are often based on the decennial census, which gradually becomes outdated, and which falls short of complete accuracy even when current. Door-to-door sampling is plagued by not–at–homes and refusals to be interviewed.[12] Telephone surveys are limited to families with listed telephones, and even many of these cannot be contacted and of those who are reached, many refuse to reply. Nonresponse in mail surveys typically runs around 80%. Thus, even with the best of intentions, it is generally not possible to obtain a random sample from the population.[13]

---

[11] Raymond A. Bauer and Stephen A. Greyser, *Advertising in America: The Consumer View*, Division of Research, Harvard Business School, 1968.

[12] According to an article in *The New York Times*, members of the Council of American Survey Research Organizations, an industry association, reported that 38% of consumers turned down requests for interviews in 1988 ("Surveys Proliferate, but Answers Dwindle," *The New York Times*, October 5, 1990).

[13] One exception, where true random sampling can be carried out, is in sampling a mailing list. In this case, the names on the list constitute the population, and from the responses of a sample of names on the list, one can make legitimate inferences about how the entire mailing list would respond.

Many polling organizations and market research agencies, nevertheless, report sample results in the form of estimates, confidence intervals, and significance tests, as if the samples that provided the data were truly random. Are such results seriously misleading? Sometimes they are.[14] But before throwing the inferential baby out with the nonrandom bathwater, it is important to understand what may go wrong when one tries to make inferences from such a nonrandom sample.

The implications of a nonrandom sample depend on the reason for the lack of randomness and the nature of the study. If you are asking about evening television viewing habits, people who are not at home in the evenings are likely to be very different from people found at home at that time. But if you are interested in which of two spaghetti sauces they prefer, it may be more reasonable to believe that at–homes can be treated as nearly, if not exactly, representative of not-at-homes. It is sometimes possible to test such a proposition by making special efforts to track down a sample of not-at-homes, but one is always left with the lingering doubt that the trackable not-at-homes are different from those who could not be tracked. And it is even harder to test whether respondents who willingly answer an interviewer's questions are representative of those who slam their doors in the interviewer's face, or hang up the telephone.

One corrective action commonly taken by sampling organizations is to replace randomly selected nonrespondents with respondents who have identical, or nearly identical, demographic profiles, such as age, gender, ethnicity, education, and income. To the extent that these demographic characteristics help to distinguish the responses of different segments of the population, this replacement technique makes sense: for example, if the young and the old have markedly different attitudes towards rock music, then replacing a young nonrespondent with an old substitute would distort your sample estimates about the population's musical tastes, while replacing the young nonrespondent with a young substitute would avoid that particular kind of distortion. Nevertheless, the replacement necessarily differs from the nonrespondent with respect to willingness to respond, and to the extent that one can hypothesize a link between willingness to respond and musical taste, a problem remains. If no such link seems plausible, then this corrective action is probably sufficient to render inferences about the population reliable.

# APPENDIX:
# ELEMENTS OF SAMPLING THEORY

## Sample Standard Deviation

*Spreadsheet Calculation.*   The sample standard deviation $s$ is a measure of how spread out the values in a sample are. If you have a column in an Excel spreadsheet consisting of the value of each sample observation, then the =STDEV function, applied to the column of sample values, gives you the sample standard deviation.

---

[14] In the famous *Literary Digest* poll of 1936 to predict the outcome of the Landon–Roosevelt presidential election, over 10 million ballots were mailed to people whose names were selected from lists of owners of telephones and automobiles. Of the 2,376,523 ballots returned, 54.5% were for Landon, the Republican candidate, who received only 36.7% of the popular vote. Subsequent analysis revealed that most of the huge error was due to the fact that people on the lists were not representative of nonowners of telephones or cars, who were much more likely to vote for the Democratic candidate.

If you want to compute the sample standard deviation without relying on the =STDEV function, go through the following steps:

- Suppose the sample values are in column A. Compute the average of the values in column A using the =AVERAGE function.
- In column B compute the difference between the first number in column A and the average of the values. This is called a **deviation**.
- In column C compute the square of the first deviation in column B.
- Now copy the computations in the first row of columns B and C to all the other sample values.
- Compute the sum of the squared deviations (column C), using the =SUM function.
- Divide this sum by $n - 1$.
- Compute the square root, using the =SQRT function. This is the sample standard deviation.

In words, the sample standard deviation $s$ is computed by taking the sum of the squared deviations, dividing by $n-1$, and taking the square root.[15]

***Standard Deviation of a Dummy Variable.*** If the values in column A are zeros and ones only, you can verify that the above procedure results in a value equal to

$$s = \sqrt{f*(1-f)*n/(n-1)}$$

where $f$ is the fraction of 1s (or the average of the values in column A).

***Degrees of Freedom.*** You may have noticed that the sample standard deviation uses a divisor of $n-1$ before you take the square root, while the standard deviation defined in Chapter 1 uses a divisor of $n$. Or, the Excel function for the standard deviation in Chapter 1 was =STDEVP, while here we are using =STDEV. Why the difference?

In Chapter 1 we were computing the mean and standard deviation of a *population*. Here, we are computing the corresponding statistics for a *sample*. The same computations are used for the population and the sample mean, but there is a slight difference (divisor of $n-1$ vs. $n$) for the sample standard deviation.

Just as the sample mean is an estimate of the population mean, the sample standard deviation is an estimate of the population standard deviation. We would like the sample mean and the sample standard deviation to be "unbiased" estimators. By this we mean that if you took repeated random samples of fixed size (say $n = 10$) with replacement (i.e., with the possibility of drawing the same element more than once in a given sample), the sample estimate would sometimes be too high and sometimes be too low, but in the long run would "average out" to the corresponding population value. The sample mean is an unbiased estimate of the population mean, but the sample standard deviation using a divisor of $n$ is not an unbiased estimate of the population standard deviation. It will "average out" too low,[16] because in order to compute the sample standard deviation, you first must compute the sample mean from the same set of data.

In statistical terminology, every one of the $n$ sample values provides a **degree of freedom** for estimating sample statistics. One degree of freedom is used to estimate the sample mean, leaving just $n - 1$ for estimating the sample standard deviation.

---

[15] Because the standard error (the standard deviation of the confidence distribution) also involves a division by $\sqrt{n}$, it is easy to become confused. Here we are talking about how to compute $s$, the sample standard deviation, which is an estimate of the population standard deviation. The **standard error**, as previously stated, is $s/\sqrt{n}$.

[16] In the extreme, if you used a sample of one height to estimate the standard deviation of the heights of first–year MBA students at Harvard Business School, your sample standard deviation, using a divisor of n, would be 0, which clearly underestimates the true value.

In order for the average value of the sample standard deviation to be approximately equal to the value of the population standard deviation, you should, instead of dividing the sum of squared deviations by $n$ (the sample size), divide by $n - 1$ (the degrees of freedom), and then take the square root. (In Excel, the =STDEV function does this for you automatically.)

Except when the sample size is very small (10 or less), this refinement is of no practical consequence, and this discussion is included merely to introduce the concept, not to plague you with additional computational burdens. However, when we come to regression, more degrees of freedom are used up in estimating additional statistics, and the degrees-of-freedom issue will become consequential.

***Finite–Population Correction.*** In this chapter we noted that the accuracy of a sample depends on its absolute size, not on its size relative to the size of the population from which it was drawn: a sample of 100 gives rise to a confidence interval of the same length, whether it was drawn from a population of 1,000 or a population of 1,000,000. That's not quite right, as you can see if you imagine a population size of 101. In that case, a sample of 100 will surely leave you far less uncertain about the value of the population mean than you would be if the population were 1,000,000.

For samples of size $n$ drawn without replacement (i.e., so that the same individual or item cannot appear more than once in the sample) from a population of size $N$, the standard error is not $s/\sqrt{n}$, but rather

$$s * \sqrt{(N-n)/(N-1)} / \sqrt{n} \quad .$$

The factor $\sqrt{(N-n)/(N-1)}$ is called the **finite–population correction**, or FPC. If $N = 1,000,000$ and $n = 100$, the FPC = 0.99995, and can be ignored. If $N = 1,000$ and $n = 100$, the FPC = 0.949, so that ignoring the FPC will result in a standard error that is only around 5% too large, and no great harm is done by ignoring it. If $N = 101$ and $n = 100$, however, the FPC = 0.1, and ignoring it would result in a standard error that is ten times too large.

In almost all practical sampling situations, you seldom sample more than 10% of the population, and ignoring the FPC does no great harm.

## Summary of Formulas

***Notation.*** $n$: sample size
$m$: sample mean
$f$: sample fraction
$s$: sample standard deviation
$c$: critical value, relative to which the significance of a sample outcome is measured

***Estimate of Population Average.*** Sample mean or average ($m$), or sample fraction ($f$).

***Confidence Intervals.*** $m - s/\sqrt{n}$ to $m + s/\sqrt{n}$ : 68% confidence ,

$m - 2s/\sqrt{n}$ to $m + 2s/\sqrt{n}$ : 95% confidence ,

$m - 3s/\sqrt{n}$ to $m + 3s/\sqrt{n}$ : 99.7% confidence .

***Statistical Significance.*** If $t = (m - c)/(s/\sqrt{n}) < -2$ or $> 2$, the sample mean differs significantly from the critical value at the 2½% level; if $t < -3$ or $> 3$, the outcome is significant at the 0.15% level.

***Sample Size.***    If you want a confidence interval of length $L$ with:

68% certainty, then $n = 4s^2/L^2$ ;

95% certainty, then $n = 16s^2/L^2$ ;

99.7% certainty, then $n = 36s^2/L^2$ .

***Computations.***    Define $x_i$ to be the value of the "*i–th*" observation, $i = 1, ..., n$. Then the following "formulas" can be used. For the Excel formulas (in italics), assume the data is in the range A1:A100.

***Sample mean (m) or fraction (f) of a dummy variable.***    Add the sample values and divide by the sample size n.

$$m = f = \frac{1}{n}\sum_{i=1}^{n} x_i$$

*=AVERAGE(A1:A100)* .

***Sample standard deviation (s).***    Subtract from each sample value its mean ($m$), and square the result. Add these squared values, divide by $n - 1$, and take the square root.

$$s = \sqrt{\frac{1}{n-1}\sum_{i=1}^{n}(x_i - m)^2}$$

*=STDEV(A1:A100)* .

If the population values are all 0s or 1s

$$s = \sqrt{f*(1-f)*n/(n-1)}$$

***Standard error.***[17]    Divide the sample standard deviation ($s$) by the square root of the sample size.

$$\text{Standard error} = s/\sqrt{n}$$

*=STDEV(A1:A100)/SQRT(100)* .

# EXERCISES ON SAMPLING AND STATISTICAL INFERENCE

1.  Several years ago, in conjunction with a computer exercise, all first-year students at Harvard Business School were asked to report their height (in inches), weight (in pounds), and gender. Data on 768 students were acquired in this fashion. The following sample of 20 weights was selected at random from the 768. (See data file HTWTSAMP.XLS on your data diskette.)

|     |     |     |     |     |
|-----|-----|-----|-----|-----|
| 160 | 113 | 140 | 148 | 185 |
| 130 | 185 | 155 | 166 | 161 |
| 158 | 200 | 144 | 180 | 210 |
| 170 | 175 | 108 | 155 | 163 |

a)  Compute the sample mean and sample standard deviation.

---

[17] There is no direct formula in Excel for calculating the standard error. However, under the Options menu, Analysis Tools command, Excel has an Add-In called Descriptive Statistics, which calculates, among other things, the mean, standard deviation, and standard error.

b)  Compute a confidence interval that has a 95% probability of covering the true average weight of the 768–person population.

c)  The average weight of the 768–person population was 154.15 pounds. Did your confidence interval cover the true average?

d)  Two people in the sample of 20 were women: one weighing 113 pounds and the other 108 pounds. Of the 768 students on which data were available, 171 were women. On the basis of this information, what is your best estimate, based on the sample, of the average population weight?

2.  The presidents at two large midwestern state universities, State University and State College, are bickering over the academic quality of their respective incoming freshman classes. Unbeknownst to either, the combined SAT scores at the two schools are as follows:

|                | STATE UNIVERSITY | STATE COLLEGE |
|----------------|------------------|---------------|
| AVERAGE        | 950              | 930           |
| STD. DEVIATION | 160              | 160           |

a)  Assume that both presidents will sample the same number of incoming freshmen at their respective schools. How large a sample do the presidents need in order to establish, with 95% confidence, that the average SAT score for State University freshmen is higher than the average SAT scores for State College freshmen?

b)  The sample has been taken, and the president of State University claims: "My students are better. The difference in average scores is statistically significant." The president of State College argues: "On average, your students may be better, but many of my students are better than many of your students." Be prepared to discuss the statistical merit of these two statements. Estimate, without calculating, the probability that a randomly selected student from State University will have a higher SAT score than a randomly selected student from State College.

3.  National Cookie Company produces premium chocolate chip cookies for sale in up–scale food markets. Cookies are sold in 250 gram packages of 10 cookies. Unfortunately, the manufacturing process has some inherent variation. After years of improving the process, National has reduced the standard deviation of the process to 0.6 grams per cookie. In the short term, the variation of the production process is outside National's control. However, National is able to adjust the mean weight level for each cookie. For various economic reasons, setting the mean level properly is important. If it is too high, then the cookies are heavier than required and National must incur unnecessarily high raw material costs; if the mean level is too low, then the cookies must be sold as thrift.

a)  Assume that National sets the maximum number of underweight packages at 2.5%. Where should National set the mean production level per cookie?

b)  Without carrying out any calculations, describe how National should determine the optimal number of underweight packages. It might be helpful to assume the following concrete numbers: raw material costs are $0.12 cents per gram, and cookies sell to distributors for $1.75 per package (regular) and $0.75 per package (thrift).

Note: solving the problem in general requires calculus.

4. The Water's Edge Company sold a variety of products related to water sports (sailing, swimming, water polo, snorkeling, etc.) by mail-order catalog. The Company's entire mailing list contained over 20,000,000 customer names and addresses. In the summer of 1990, they decided to run an experiment to ascertain which of two catalog formats would draw more customers. Accordingly, they sent out a sample of 500,000 issues in their standard 7½-by-8½-inch format, and another sample of 500,000 in an experimental 8½-by-11-inch format. The two customer groups of 500,000 were chosen so as to match one another as closely as possible with respect to past purchasing behavior and geographical location. The standard catalog was sent to the 19,000,000 other customers, but responses from the experimental mailings could be identified by the item numbers that customers used to specify merchandise ordered, which were unique to those catalogs. Orders generated by the catalogs were as follows:

> STANDARD:          8,450   or   1.69%
>
> EXPERIMENTAL:     11,472   or   2.29%

   a) Construct 99.7% confidence intervals for the percent in their entire mailing list who would respond to each of the two catalog formats. Do the confidence intervals overlap? What can you infer about the difference in response rates for the two formats in the entire population?

   b) Would you use the experimental 8½-by-11–inch format in your new catalogs? Why or why not?

   c) Before running the experiment, there had been some discussion of simply sending the experimental version of the catalog to all 20,000,000 customers, and comparing the 1990 response rate with that of 1989. List the pros and cons of this method versus the experimental method actually used.

5. The following exercise is designed to demonstrate that confidence intervals can be interpreted as probability statements about a population mean. You will be asked to "sample" three variables, for each of which there are 768 observations in data file HTWT.XLS, which was distributed to you on your data diskette. From the samples, you will compute confidence intervals and determine whether or not those intervals cover the true mean of the population.

   The three variables in question are height, weight, and gender. As you can easily verify, the average height of all 768 students is 69.52 inches, the average weight is 154.15 pounds, and the "average gender" is 0.223 (male students were coded 0 and females 1, but the average is simply the fraction of female students in the population).

   You will be asked to take a sample of 20 students' heights, a sample of another 20 students' weights, and a sample of still another 20 genders, and compute confidence intervals from those three samples. You could do the sampling by putting 768 slips of paper, numbered 1 through 768, into a hat, drawing 20 such slips, for each slip finding the student in the list corresponding to that number, writing down the value of the appropriate variable, and computing a confidence interval based on the sample you had drawn.

Fortunately, Excel has a much less tedious mechanism for accomplishing the same task. Here's what you should do:

▸ Open the file HTWT.XLS.

▸ Click the **Tools** menu, then **Data Analysis**, then **Random Number Generation.**

▸ When the dialog box appears, click on **3** for Number of Variables, **20** for Number of Random Numbers, select **Uniform** for Distribution, and type[18] **1** and **769** in the two boxes designated as Between. Under Output Options, click on Output Range and type G7 in the corresponding box.

If you were to click OK, you would see three columns of 20 random numbers uniformly distributed between 1 and 769; however, your numbers would be the same as everyone else's. As we want each student to create a different set of samples, there is one more step: you must supply a number in the box labeled Random Seed. To ensure that each of you has a unique (or nearly unique) random seed, please enter your birthday in the form ddmmy, where dd contains the one or two digits of the day of the month in which you were born, mm is a two-digit representation of the month (January = 01, February = 02, ..., December = 12), and **y** is the last digit of the year in which you were born. Here is how you would designate the random seed for various birthdays:

| | |
|---|---|
| January 2, 1968 | 2018 |
| July 17, 1966 | 17076 |
| December 31, 1960 | 31120 |

▸ Enter this four- or five-digit number in the box labeled Random Seed, and click **OK**.

Now, to obtain the random sample:

▸ Place the cursor on cell **G28** (two rows below the bottom of the first column of random numbers).

▸ Type the formula **=INDEX(C$7:C$774,G7)** and press **Enter**. (Be careful to enter the $ signs exactly as shown.) If the random number in cell G7 was equal to or greater than 1, but less than 2, the number in G28 will be the first height listed in column C; if it was equal to or greater than 2, but less than 3, it will be the second, etc. Thus each of the 768 heights has an equal chance to be selected.

▸ Copy the formula in G28 down through row 47, and across to Column I, so that 20 rows and 3 columns are filled with sample observations. Those in Column G are sample heights, in H sample weights, and in I sample genders.

Now, for each of these three columns, compute the sample average, the sample standard deviation, the standard error, and a 68% confidence interval. Determine whether each of the three intervals covers the true average. Please bring printouts of all your computations to class. Among other things, your professor should check in class to see what fraction of 68% confidence intervals covered the true average.

---

[18] We really mean 769, not 768. The idea here is that every number produced, rounded down to the nearest integer, will be an integer between 1 and 768. For each random number drawn, each integer between 1 and 768 has a probability 1/768 of being selected.

# TIME SERIES

## INTRODUCTION

A time series consists of observations on a single variable at discrete points in time, usually at equal intervals. Typical time series may involve:

- Elements of the national income and product accounts at yearly, quarterly, or monthly intervals (Gross domestic product, government spending, consumer price index, unemployment rate, etc.)
- Measures appropriate to individual business operations (monthly sales, machine efficiencies, defect rate, etc.)
- Financial market statistics (daily closing price of IBM stock)
- Meteorological data (daily high temperatures in Boston, monthly amount of precipitation in Chicago)
- Population data (U.S. population, or births, or deaths by year)

The order of the observations is an essential characteristic of each of these series.

We have already seen that some time series may exhibit trends and seasonals. For example, monthly retail sales in the United States are characterized by an upward trend and a pronounced seasonal, with a sharp peak in December and a trough in January and February. The upward trend may be explained, in part, by other time series: population growth, per-capita income growth, or inflation, for example. Fluctuations from the trend and seasonal effects may be explained, in part, as the effects of weather, consumer confidence, availability of credit, etc. Thus, it is quite natural to "explain" the behavior of a particular time series in terms of trend, seasonal, and the effects of other variables that are themselves time series. Unfortunately, those other variables, while potentially useful in explaining past values, may not be useful in predicting future values of the time series in which we are interested. For example, while bad weather may have reduced retail sales last month, unless we have a reliable forecast of the weather for next month, weather is not a useful variable for predicting future sales.[1]

Harvard Business School note 9-893-012. This note was prepared by Professor Arthur Schleifer, Jr.
Copyright © 1993 by the President and Fellows of Harvard College.

[1] There are three important cases in which explanatory variables *should* be used in forecasting future values of a time series. First, if the explanatory variable is a "leading indicator" its value will be known in advance: permits for housing starts may be good predictors of refrigerator sales a year later. Second, some variables can be forecast with accuracy because their values can be controlled by the firm: changes in price, advertising expenditures, or packaging may contemporaneously affect sales of a product, but a company's decision to effect such changes will be known to a company forecaster in advance. Third, some explanatory variables may be more easily or accurately predicted than the time series in question: although their actual values will not be known in advance, their forecast values will. In effect, variables of this sort are like leading indicators. Although forecasts of elements of the national income and products accounts are subject to error, they may be much more accurate than forecasts of your company's sales, because professional forecasting organizations have devoted great effort to developing appropriate prediction models.

Because current values of explanatory variables are not always useful in predicting future values of a time series, forecasters are often restricted to looking at the information within the series itself, without relying on other explanatory variables. There is considerable information embedded in such series: we have seen that trends tend to continue and seasonal patterns tend to repeat. Thus it's a safe bet to predict that next January's retail sales will be substantially less than those of the preceding month, and it's probably reasonable to predict that they will exceed the preceding January's sales.

What if we have a time series with no discernible trend or seasonal?[2] Is there any information in the time series itself that will help us to predict its value in future periods? The answer is "Yes," but it takes some analysis to extract this information. We can think of the observations that constitute the time series as a sample from a process that generates data according to some (probabilistic) rule. We seek ways of using the sample data to identify the rule that governs the data-generating process. If we know what the rule is, we can then make (probabilistic) forecasts of future values of the time series.

The number of rules that could give rise to time series observed in the real world—even those with no trend or seasonal—is huge, and any attempt to cover the subject of time-series analysis in all of its richness requires a book, not a chapter. The purpose of this chapter is to introduce you to the concept of time-series analysis and to introduce two very simple rules for generating data that describe the way some important time series behave in the real world. At the end of this chapter, we'll give an indication of where and how this subject unfolds, but for now we shall introduce the two rules, then show how time-series data generated by one or the other of these rules can be identified and analyzed, and how appropriate forecasts can be made.

# CONCEPTS USED IN DATA GENERATION RULES

## Notation

We shall measure time at periods denoted by 1, 2, ..., $t$, ..., $T$. For example, period 1 might be midnight on January 1, period 2 might be midnight on January 2, etc. If we had a year's worth of data, $T$ would be 365. Let's denote the value of the time series at time $t$ by $y_t$: in the example above, the first observation (the value of the series on January 1) will be denoted by $y_1$, the last by $y_{365}$. We shall refer to the entire time series (one year's worth of daily data in the example above) as $Y_t$; the reason for the subscript $t$ will become clear in a moment. Because the rule generating the time series is probabilistic—meaning that we won't be able to forecast the next value of the series with certainty—we need to introduce the notion of a random "disturbance" at time $t$, denoted by $e_t$. Each disturbance is, by definition, drawn from the same probability distribution, and its value doesn't depend on the value of any prior disturbances. (This definition is summarized by saying that the values of $e_t$ are **independent** and **identically distributed**, sometimes abbreviated **iid**.)

---

[2] The assumptions of no explanatory variables, no trend, and no seasonal are less restrictive than they might appear to be. Even when we are analyzing time series that can be explained or predicted via trends, seasonals, or other explanatory variables, we are often interested in knowing what information, if any, is left in the series after these explanatory factors have been taken into consideration.

It is convenient to specify that the mean of $e_t$ is 0. Thus, $e_t$ could be +1 with probability 0.5 and –1 with probability 0.5; or it could be + 2 with probability 0.3, 0 with probability 0.1, and –1 with probability 0.6. Usually, we will specify simply that et has a normal distribution with mean 0 and some fixed standard deviation S—say S = 2.5.

## Autocorrelation

A concept indispensable to the analysis of time series is **autocorrelation**. We have already looked at the idea of correlation between two variables, say $x$ and $y$: we can estimate the correlation between $x$ and $y$ by plotting a scatter diagram; we can measure it by computing the correlation coefficient.

In time-series analysis, there is only one variable, but we can easily create new variables consisting of the old variable lagged one or more periods. If $Y_t$ represents the original series, consisting of observations $y_1, y_2, ..., y_t, ..., y_T$ , then $Y_{t-1}$ will represent the same series lagged one period. If there are no observations prior to period 1, then the first value of $Y_{t-1}$ will be missing, but the second will be $y_1$, the third $y_2$, and the last $y_{T-1}$. If the original series $Y_t$ consisted of daily observations for a year, starting January 1 and ending December 31, then $Y_{t-1}$ would have a missing first observation, its second observation would be the value of the series on January 1, and its last observation would be the value on December 30.

We thus have two variables, $Y_t$ and $Y_{t-1}$, derived from a single time series. We can plot a scatter diagram of the two variables (only $T–1$ points can be plotted), and we can compute the coefficient of correlation between $Y_t$ and $Y_{t-1}$. This coefficient is called the (first-order) **autocorrelation coefficient**.

There is no reason to restrict our analysis to one-period lags. A variable $Y_{t-2}$ would start with two missing observations; the third observation would be the value of the series on January 1, and the last would be the value on December 29. A scatter diagram of $Y_t$ versus $Y_{t-2}$ would reveal whether there was any substantial second-order correlation, and the second-order autocorrelation coefficient would quantify it.

# TWO DATA-GENERATING RULES

## The Constant-Average Rule

One of the simplest rules by which a time series can be generated is the constant-average rule, which specifies that each value of the series is the sum of a constant, $M$, plus a disturbance; for the $t^{th}$ observation,

$$y_t = M + e_t .$$

Neither $M$ nor the values of $e_t$ are directly observable, but inferences about them can be made by analyzing the data.

***Simulating the Series.*** What does a constant-average series look like? We can artificially simulate such a series by specifying a value for $M$, a probability distribution for $e_t$, and then drawing sample disturbances from this distribution. Suppose $M = 10$, $T = 20$, and $e_t$ has a normal distribution with mean 0, standard deviation 2.5. Values of $e_t$ should be such that each value is independent of prior values; in the long run, the average value should be 0, 68% of the values should be between –2.5 and + 2.5, 95% between –5 and + 5, 99.7% between –7.5 and + 7.5, the histogram should look appropriately bell-shaped, and the cumugram should be appropriately S-shaped.[3] Of course, in any sample, the actual values of $e_t$ will fail to conform exactly to these criteria because of sampling error.

The first four columns of Table 3.1 shows values of the variable $Y_t$ generated in this way. Figure 3.1 shows values of $Y_t$ plotted as a time series.

**Table 3.1**

| $t$ | $M$ | $e_t$ | $Y_t$ | $Y_{t-1}$ | $Y_{t-2}$ | $Y_{t-3}$ | $Y_{t-4}$ | $Y_{t-5}$ |
|---|---|---|---|---|---|---|---|---|
| 1 | 10 | 0.33 | 10.33 | | | | | |
| 2 | 10 | 2.25 | 12.25 | 10.33 | | | | |
| 3 | 10 | 0.22 | 10.22 | 12.25 | 10.33 | | | |
| 4 | 10 | 0.13 | 10.13 | 10.22 | 12.25 | 10.33 | | |
| 5 | 10 | 0.70 | 10.70 | 10.13 | 10.22 | 12.25 | 10.33 | |
| 6 | 10 | −1.43 | 8.57 | 10.70 | 10.13 | 10.22 | 12.25 | 10.33 |
| 7 | 10 | 1.38 | 11.38 | 8.57 | 10.70 | 10.13 | 10.22 | 12.25 |
| 8 | 10 | 2.04 | 12.04 | 11.38 | 8.57 | 10.70 | 10.13 | 10.22 |
| 9 | 10 | 2.69 | 12.69 | 12.04 | 11.38 | 8.57 | 10.70 | 10.13 |
| 10 | 10 | 7.02 | 17.02 | 12.69 | 12.04 | 11.38 | 8.57 | 10.70 |
| 11 | 10 | −2.03 | 7.97 | 17.02 | 12.69 | 12.04 | 11.38 | 8.57 |
| 12 | 10 | −1.36 | 8.64 | 7.97 | 17.02 | 12.69 | 12.04 | 11.38 |
| 13 | 10 | 0.58 | 10.58 | 8.64 | 7.97 | 17.02 | 12.69 | 12.04 |
| 14 | 10 | −0.55 | 9.45 | 10.58 | 8.64 | 7.97 | 17.02 | 12.69 |
| 15 | 10 | −2.29 | 7.71 | 9.45 | 10.58 | 8.64 | 7.97 | 17.02 |
| 16 | 10 | 0.37 | 10.37 | 7.71 | 9.45 | 10.58 | 8.64 | 7.97 |
| 17 | 10 | 1.88 | 11.88 | 10.37 | 7.71 | 9.45 | 10.58 | 8.64 |
| 18 | 10 | −0.58 | 9.42 | 11.88 | 10.37 | 7.71 | 9.45 | 10.58 |
| 19 | 10 | −2.49 | 7.51 | 9.42 | 11.88 | 10.37 | 7.71 | 9.45 |
| 20 | 10 | 4.35 | 14.35 | 7.51 | 9.42 | 11.88 | 10.37 | 7.71 |
| | | | | **Autocorrelation Coefficients** | | | | |
| Mean | | | 10.66 | −0.025 | −0.213 | −0.110 | −0.139 | −0.292 |
| Std. Dev. | | | 2.32 | | | | | |
| Std. Error | | | 0.52 | | | | | |

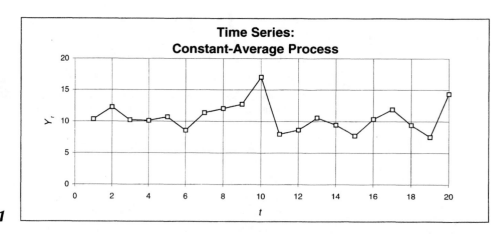

**Figure 3.1**

---

[3] There are many mechanical ways of drawing random disturbances that have these characteristics, but by far the easiest is to use the Excel 5.0 facility available by clicking Tools, Data Analysis, Random Number Generation, and specifying that the distribution is normal, that the mean is 0, the standard deviation is 2.5, and the number of random variables is 20 (the value of $T$).

***Identifying the Rule.*** Now let's switch gears. Suppose we were presented with the 20 observations on $Y_t$ given in Table 3.1. If we knew what those observations represented, we might be able to identify the rule governing the data-generating process. For now we will simply ask how, by examining the data, could we check a hypothesis that those observations came from a constant-average process?

If that hypothesis were true, each observation would differ from $M$ by an amount that does not depend on the value of the previous observation. Therefore, a scatter diagram of each observation plotted against its predecessor should show no correlation (except for sampling error). In column 5 of Table 3.1 we show $Y_{t-1}$, the values of $Y_t$ lagged by one period.[4] Figure 3.2 is a scatter diagram, showing values of $Y_{t-1}$ on the horizontal axis and values of $Y_t$ on the vertical. There is no discernible correlation. The coefficient of correlation between $Y_t$ and $Y_{t-1}$ (the first-order autocorrelation coefficient), based on the 19 observations for which both variables have values, is $-0.025$; it is printed at the bottom of the fifth column in Table 3.1. We have not introduced the specific technique for computing the confidence distribution of a correlation coefficient, but it can be shown that when the population correlation coefficient is 0 and the sample size is 19, a 68% confidence interval will cover sample correlation coefficients between $-0.24$ and $+0.24$, and a 95% interval will cover $-0.45$ to $+0.45$; thus the observed sample correlation coefficient of $-0.025$ is by no means inconsistent with the hypothesis that in a sufficiently large sample, $Y_t$ and $Y_{t-1}$ would be uncorrelated.

**Figure 3.2**

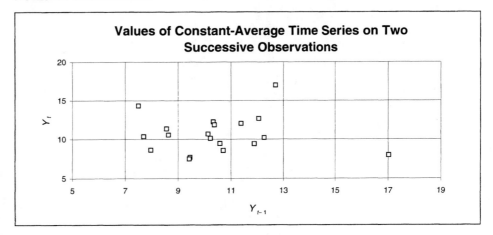

We could now go on to create new variables consisting of two-period lags $Y_{t-2}$, three-period lags $Y_{t-3}$, etc., and for each of these compute the appropriate-order sample autocorrelation coefficient: a second-order coefficient based on the correlation between $Y_t$ and $Y_{t-2}$, a third-order coefficient, etc. These coefficients are computed up to five-period lags, and are shown at the bottoms of their appropriate columns in Table 3.1. As we would expect, they are sufficiently close to 0 to be consistent with a hypothesis that process autocorrelation coefficients of all orders are 0. This is the key to identifying a time series as one generated by a constant-average rule: for such a series, *sample autocorrelation coefficients of all orders will differ from 0 only because of sampling error.*

---

[4] These values are easily obtained in Excel 5.0 by copying the value of $y_1$ into an adjacent column one row down, and then dragging the Fill handle down.

***Forecasting.***    Having identified the rule that governed the generation of the data, we can now try to make a forecast. If we knew that $M = 10$, and that the disturbances were normally distributed with mean 0, standard deviation $S = 2.5$, a "point" forecast for $y_{21}$ would be 10, and a probabilistic forecast would be between 7.5 and 12.5 with probability 0.68, between 5.0 and 15.0 with probability 0.95, and between 2.5 and 17.5 with probability 0.997. Unfortunately, we don't know the value of $M$, the standard deviation of the disturbances, or even that the disturbances are normally distributed. But the data provide *estimates* of $M$ and $S$: the sample mean $m = 10.66$ is not very far from the process mean $M = 10$; and the sample standard deviation $s = 2.32$ is not very far from the process standard deviation $S = 2.5$. If the disturbances were normally distributed, then the values of $y_t$ in the sample of 20 observations should be approximately normally distributed; that this is so can be verified by plotting a cumugram of the actual values of $y_t$ and of a normal distribution with mean of 10.66, standard deviation of 2.32. Figure 3.3 shows such a plot; the fit is quite good.[5]

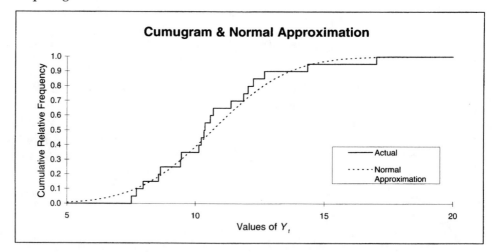

***Figure 3.3***

We can now either use the cumugram of actual values to make probabilistic forecasts or, more simply, use the normal approximation. Using the latter, we would get approximate probability intervals as follows: the value of $y_{21}$ would be between 8.34 and 12.98 with probability 0.68; between 6.02 and 15.30 with probability 0.95; and between 3.70 and 17.62 with probability 0.997. These intervals are close to, but not exactly the same as, the ones we computed assuming we knew the values of $M$ and $S$ and the rule that governed the data-generating process for sure. In general, intervals computed in this way from sample data will be too narrow, on the average, because we have made four simplifying assumptions:

1.    We are using the sample mean $m$ instead of the process mean $M$.

2.    We are using the sample standard deviation $s$ instead of the process standard deviation $S$.

---

[5] Normal cumugram values corresponding to any given value of $y$ can be computed by the Excel function NORMDIST($y,m,s$,1).

3. We are assuming the disturbances are normally distributed, an assumption supported by, but not proved by, Figure 3.3.

4. We are assuming that the rule that governed the data-generating process was a constant-average rule, which is supported by, but not proved by, the autocorrelation analysis.

More sophisticated methods can make adjustments to take into account the first two simplifying assumptions, but only judgment can adjust for the third and fourth. For our purposes, just understanding that the intervals are somewhat too narrow is sufficient.

Suppose we want to forecast $y_{22}$, the value of $y$ two periods ahead. If we knew the value of $y_{21}$, the value of $y$ one period ahead, we could recompute $m$ and $s$ based on all 21 observations, and compute a point forecast and probabilistic forecasts based on these new statistics. But if we have only 20 observations in hand, and are looking two periods ahead, all we can do is use the values of $m$ and $s$ that are based on 20 observations: the forecasts for $y_{22}$ and subsequent values of $y$ are precisely the same as that for $y_{21}$.

There are thus two important characteristics of constant-average rules: both point forecasts and probabilistic forecasts of future values, no matter how far into the future, are all precisely the same; and all existing observations are equally important in determining forecasts of future values. The value of $y_1$ is as important in forecasting the value of $y_{21}$ as is the value of $y_{20}$. As we shall see, these characteristics of constant-average rules do not apply to the next rule that we shall consider.

## The Random-Walk Rule

A time-series observation generated by a random-walk rule is equal to its immediate predecessor plus a random disturbance:

$$y_t = y_{t-1} + e_t \ .$$

If the first observation is $y_0$, then

$$y_1 = y_0 + e_1 \ ,$$

and

$$y_2 = y_1 + e_2 \ ,$$

etc. Unlike the constant-mean rule, the values of the disturbances $e_1$ through $e_T$ are observable.

***Simulating the Series.*** What does a random-walk series look like? We can artificially simulate such a series by specifying a starting value for $y_0$, a probability distribution for $e_t$, and then drawing sample disturbances from this distribution. Suppose $y_0 = 10$, $T = 20$, and $e_t$ has a normal distribution with mean 0, standard deviation 2.5. The first three columns of Table 3.2 show values of the variable $Y_t$ generated in this way. Figure 3.4 on the following page shows values of $Y_t$ plotted as a time series.

**Table 3.2**

| $t$ | $e_t$ | $Y_t$ | $e_{t-1}$ | $e_{t-2}$ | $e_{t-3}$ | $e_{t-4}$ | $Y_{t-1}$ |
|---|---|---|---|---|---|---|---|
| 0 | | 10.00 | | | | | |
| 1 | 0.33 | 10.33 | | | | | 10.00 |
| 2 | 2.25 | 12.58 | 0.33 | | | | 10.33 |
| 3 | 0.22 | 12.81 | 2.25 | 0.33 | | | 12.58 |
| 4 | 0.13 | 12.94 | 0.22 | 2.25 | 0.33 | | 12.81 |
| 5 | 0.70 | 13.64 | 0.13 | 0.22 | 2.25 | 0.33 | 12.94 |
| 6 | −1.43 | 12.20 | 0.70 | 0.13 | 0.22 | 2.25 | 13.64 |
| 7 | 1.38 | 13.58 | −1.43 | 0.70 | 0.13 | 0.22 | 12.20 |
| 8 | 2.04 | 15.63 | 1.38 | −1.43 | 0.70 | 0.13 | 13.58 |
| 9 | 2.69 | 18.32 | 2.04 | 1.38 | −1.43 | 0.70 | 15.63 |
| 10 | 7.02 | 25.34 | 2.69 | 2.04 | 1.38 | −1.43 | 18.32 |
| 11 | −2.03 | 23.31 | 7.02 | 2.69 | 2.04 | 1.38 | 25.34 |
| 12 | −1.36 | 21.95 | −2.03 | 7.02 | 2.69 | 2.04 | 23.31 |
| 13 | 0.58 | 22.53 | −1.36 | −2.03 | 7.02 | 2.69 | 21.95 |
| 14 | −0.55 | 21.98 | 0.58 | −1.36 | −2.03 | 7.02 | 22.53 |
| 15 | −2.29 | 19.69 | −0.55 | 0.58 | −1.36 | −2.03 | 21.98 |
| 16 | 0.37 | 20.06 | −2.29 | −0.55 | 0.58 | −1.36 | 19.69 |
| 17 | 1.88 | 21.93 | 0.37 | −2.29 | −0.55 | 0.58 | 20.06 |
| 18 | −0.58 | 21.35 | 1.88 | 0.37 | −2.29 | −0.55 | 21.93 |
| 19 | −2.49 | 18.86 | −0.58 | 1.88 | 0.37 | −2.29 | 21.35 |
| 20 | 4.35 | 23.21 | −2.49 | −0.58 | 1.88 | 0.37 | 18.86 |

| | | | **Autocorrelation Coefficients** | | | | |
|---|---|---|---|---|---|---|---|
| **Mean** | 0.66 | | −0.025 | −0.213 | 0.110 | −0.139 | 0.881 |
| **Std. Dev.** | 2.32 | | | | | | |
| **Std. Error** | 0.53 | | | | | | |

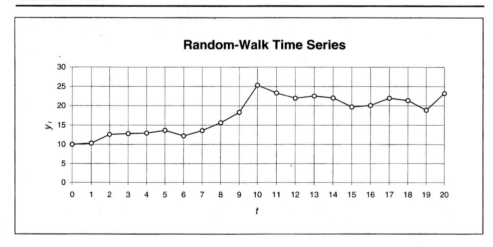

**Figure 3.4**

***Identifying the Rule*** Given the 21 observations $y_0$ through $y_{20}$ shown in Table 3.2, can we see whether a hypothesis that the observations were generated by a random-walk rule is consistent with the data? An immediate consequence of the rule

$$y_t = y_{t-1} + e_t$$

is that

$$y_t - y_{t-1} = e_t \ .$$

The difference between each observation and its immediate predecessor (often called the first difference) is just a random disturbance. Thus, first differences behave as if they were generated by a constant-mean rule with $M = 0$.

We already know how to analyze data generated by a constant-mean rule: we look at lags of one, two, and more periods, and compute sample first-order, second-order, and higher-order autocorrelation coefficients. Here the lags are not on the values of the series, but on their first differences. If the autocorrelations on these first differences can be shown to be equal to 0 except for sampling error, then the first differences are consistent with a hypothesis that they were generated by a constant-mean rule, and therefore the values of $Y_t$ are consistent with a hypothesis that they were generated by a random-walk rule.

In columns 4–7 of Table 3.2 we show lagged first differences. (Column 2 shows values of the first difference itself.) At the bottom of columns 4–7 are the autocorrelation coefficients for the first differences. Just as was true in the analysis of the constant-average process, sample autocorrelation coefficients ought to be between –0.24 and + 0.24 with confidence 68% if the process had zero autocorrelation; all the coefficients are within that interval.

In Figure 3.5 we plot first differences lagged one period against "this period's" first differences. There is no discernible correlation in the scatter diagram. Notice, however, that if we plot the lagged values of $Y_{t-1}$, given in column 8 of Table 3.2, against current values of the series itself ($Y_t$), as in Figure 3.6, there is considerable correlation. (The correlation coefficient for one-period lags is 0.881.) Contrast this with the corresponding scatter diagram for the constant-average process.

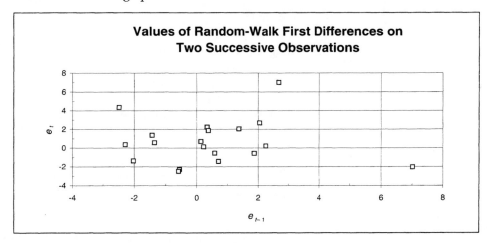

**Figure 3.5**

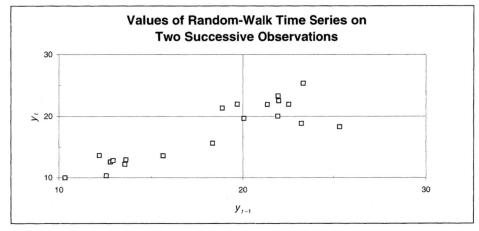

**Figure 3.6**

***Forecasting***    If we know the values of $y$ from $y_0$ through $y_{20}$, what is our best forecast for $y_{21}$? If we know that the data-generating process is a random walk, then

$$y_{21} = y_{20} + e_{21} \ .$$

Because the mean of $e_{21} = 0$, the best point forecast for $y_{21}$ is just the preceding value, $y_{20}$: the history of the process prior to the 20th observation is irrelevant to forecasts of the future. The same is true for point forecasts for $y_{22}$ and subsequent $y$'s: the best forecast is the last observed value.

Turning to probabilistic forecasts, $y_{21}$ differs from $y_{20}$ by the disturbance $e_{21}$. All the disturbances have been assumed to be independently and identically distributed. We can infer their distribution from a histogram or cumugram of their values (they are just the values of the first differences themselves) or, if we assume the disturbances are normally distributed with mean 0, we can estimate the standard deviation of the distribution by computing the sample standard deviation of the disturbances. For the data in Table 3.2, the standard deviation is 2.32. Thus, since $y_{20} = 23.21$, a probabilistic forecast for $y_{21}$ is between 20.89 and 25.53 with probability 68%, between 18.57 and 27.85 with probability 95%, etc. As was true in the case of the constant-mean process, these intervals are somewhat too narrow, for all the same reasons.

A probabilistic forecast for $y_{22}$ is a bit trickier. We know that

$$y_{22} = y_{21} + e_{22} \ ,$$

and that

$$y_{21} = y_{20} + e_{21} \ ,$$

from which it follows that

$$y_{22} = y_{20} + e_{21} + e_{22} \ .$$

What is the distribution of the sum of two iid disturbances? It can be shown that if each disturbance has a normal distribution, the sum also has a normal distribution. Furthermore, the mean of the sum is the sum of the means, or 0, and the standard deviation of the sum is $s\sqrt{2}$, where $s$ is an estimate of the standard deviation of the distribution of any one disturbance.[6] Thus a forecast for $y_{22}$ will lie in the interval $y_{20} \pm s\sqrt{2}$ with probability 68%, etc. For the data in Table 3.2, $y_{22}$ will be between 19.96 and 26.46 with probability 68%, between 10.20 and 29.72 with probability 95%, etc.

These results can be generalized. If the last observed value in a random walk is $y_T$, then a probabilistic forecast of $y_{T+n}$ will have mean $y_T$ and standard deviation $s\sqrt{n}$: the further into the future you forecast, the greater your uncertainty.

---

[6] This follows from the fact that the standard deviation of the *mean* of a sample of size 2 is $s/\sqrt{2}$, and the *sum* of a sample of size 2 is just two times the mean.

## Summary

These results are summarized in Table 3.3 below:

**Table 3.3**

|  | **Constant Mean** | **Random-Walk** |
|---|---|---|
| Process | $y_t = M + e_t$ | $y_t = y_{t-1} + e_t$ |
| Identification | All autocorrelation coefficients are 0, except for sampling error. | All autocorrelation coefficients of first differences are 0, except for sampling error. |
| **Probabilistic Forecast** *n* **Periods Ahead*** | | |
| Mean | $m$ (average of observed $y$'s) | $y_t$ (the last observed value of $y$) |
| Standard Deviation | $s$ (sample standard deviation of the observed $y$'s) | $s \sqrt{n}$ (where $s$ is the sample standard deviation of the first differences) |

* If the distribution of the disturbances is normal, then the forecast distribution is also normal.

# WHAT COMES NEXT?

We have discussed just two of the most important data-generating rules, shown how time series generated by these rules can be identified from data, and how point and probabilistic forecasts can be made. There are many other rules that generate time series that occur in practice. We are not going to investigate them in this chapter. Instead, we shall next turn to the analysis of time series—often series with trends and seasonals—where explanatory variables can be used to forecast future values. But before leaving the subject of forecasting without explanatory variables, let's take a brief look at how this subject would unfold if it were pursued further.

Having investigated constant-average and random-walk rules, the next kind of rule that would be worth exploring would be one where the (unobserved) average is not constant, but changes over time in random-walk fashion, and where the actual values of the series differ from this "moving" average by an iid disturbance. This rule for generating data is called a **moving-average rule**. It can be identified by examining the autocorrelations of first differences, and point forecasts can be made by constructing a weighted average of past observations, the weights being heaviest for the most recent observation, and declining "exponentially" for successively less recent observations. This forecasting mechanism is called **exponential smoothing**, a very robust technique that works quite well even for time series generated by rules that are not strictly of the moving-average variety.

Although we have restricted our attention to time series without trends or seasonals, we can take a "moving-average" time series and add to it a moving-average trend, and even a moving-average seasonal. Future values of such a series can be forecast by more complex exponential-smoothing techniques which smooth the seasonal, the trend, and the series itself. These techniques are often successfully applied to series generated by rules that are not strictly of the moving-average type.

A still more general and complicated set of data-generating rules assumes that each observation (or first difference) is a weighted sum of previous observations (or differences) plus a disturbance plus a weighted sum of previous disturbances.

Such processes can be identified by examining autocorrelations of the series, or of first differences, and formulas for forecasting future values are available. This very general time-series approach was pioneered by George E. P. Box and Gwilym Jenkins,[7] and is referred to as Box-Jenkins or ARIMA (Auto-Regressive Integrated Moving Average) methodology. The interested reader can find further discussion of these techniques in S. Makridakis, S. C. Wheelwright, and V. E. McGee, *Forecasting: Methods and Applications*, Second Edition. John Wiley and Sons, 1983.

## EXERCISES ON TIME SERIES

1.  Figure 3.7 shows annual average temperature in Boston from 1944 through 1990. The data are in worksheet BOSTEMP in workbook TIMSEREX.XLS. Given this set of data alone, forecast the annual average temperature for 1991 and 1992. How sure are you of your forecasts? What would your forecast and your forecast uncertainty be for 1993? Can you detect any evidence of global warming in the data?

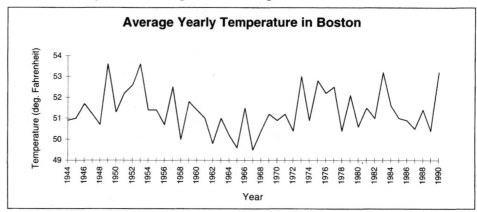

**Figure 3.7**

2.  Figure 3.8 gives the end-of-month price of gold (dollars per troy ounce on the CMX) in monthly intervals from December 31, 1981, through November 30, 1992. The data are in worksheet GOLD in workbook TIMSEREX.XLS. Given this set of data alone, what would your forecast of gold price be for the end of December 1992? How sure are you of your forecast? What would your forecast and your forecast uncertainty be for December 1993?

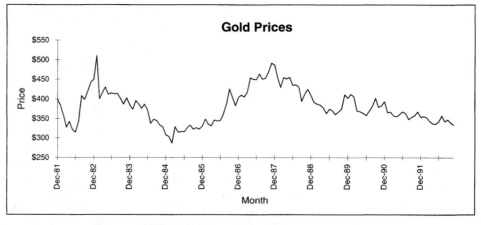

**Figure 3.8**

---

[7] G.E.P. Box, G. Jenkins, and G.C. Reinsel, *Time Series Analysis, Forecasting, and Control,* third edition. Englewood Cliffs, NJ: Prentice Hall, 1994.

# FORECASTING WITH REGRESSION ANALYSIS

Regression analysis[1] provides a powerful tool for developing forecasts of the future based on data from the past. It specifies the relationship between a variable of interest (the dependent variable) and other variables (the independent variables), and thus enables you to forecast a future value of the dependent variable when the values of the independent variables are known. In this chapter we discuss several ways of using observations of past values of a variable (and perhaps other "explanatory" variables as well) to make forecasts of its future values.

## INDISTINGUISHABLE AND DISTINGUISHABLE DATA

### ▼ Forecasting Based on "Indistinguishable" Data

The following problem illustrates how data on past observations can be used to generate a forecast of some future observation. Imagine that you are interested in selling your house. To help you forecast its selling price, you obtain a sample (shown in Table 4.1) of the selling prices of ten houses sold in your city over the past year.

Let's assume that housing prices have remained stable over the last year, and that any house in your sample is as likely to be representative of the selling price of your house as any other—your house is **indistinguishable** from the houses in your sample. Then the selling prices of those houses would be relevant to your forecasting problem. Indeed, if you wanted to make a **probabilistic** forecast of your house's selling price, in the context of a decision problem, you would simply use the **frequency distribution** of the ten selling prices in your sample.

Quite often, however, we do not have a well-defined decision problem in mind, and want just a single number—a "point forecast" or "best guess." In terms of the original sample data, you might choose a central value such as the mean, median, or mode. The central value that we use in regression is the mean.[2]

**Table 4.1**

**Selling Prices of a Sample of Ten Houses**

| |
|---|
| $109,360 |
| $137,980 |
| $131,230 |
| $130,230 |
| $125,410 |
| $124,370 |
| $139,030 |
| $140,160 |
| $144,220 |
| $154,190 |

Harvard Business School note 9-894-007. This note was prepared by Professor Arthur Schleifer, Jr. Copyright © 1993 by the President and Fellows of Harvard College.

---

[1] Other uses of regression analysis are discussed in Chapter 5.

[2] If we define a **residual** as the difference between a point forecast and an actual value, then (see the Appendix to Chapter 1) the mean minimizes the sum of squared residuals–it is a **least-squares** estimate. Regression estimates are also least-squares estimates, as we shall see.

The mean of your sample of ten houses is $133,618. How good an estimate is that? If all the prices in your sample were close to $133,618, you would feel quite confident that the selling price of your house would be in the vicinity of $133,618. You would be much less confident if the prices in your sample were widely dispersed. The sample standard deviation is a useful measure of dispersion, and serves as a benchmark relative to which other forecasting techniques can be compared. In this case, the sample standard deviation is $12,406.

## Forecasting When the Data Are Distinguishable

Now suppose that your sample contains information not just on selling prices but also on the square footage of the ten houses, as in Table 4.2. The sample no longer represents houses that are indistinguishable: larger houses are **distinguishable** from smaller houses. If your house has 1,682 square feet of living area, it seems reasonable to confine your attention to "look-alike" houses. While no house in the sample is a perfect "look-alike," there are four houses that are more than 1,600 and less than 1,800 square feet, whose selling prices, you might conjecture, would be more like the selling price of your house than those that are much smaller or much larger. The average selling price of those four houses is $132,243, slightly less than the average across all ten houses, and the sample standard deviation is $8,513, less than the sample standard deviation for all ten houses. By restricting our attention to a subset of the data consisting of houses that are nearly indistinguishable look-alikes, we have slightly refined our point forecast, and have somewhat increased its accuracy.

In Table 4.3, we show the sample average and standard deviation for all ten houses, and then similar measures for three subsets of the data (or "cells") classified by size ranges. As you can see, the sample average goes up as size increases. For all three cells, the sample standard deviation is lower than it was when we looked at all ten houses together.

## Sample Residuals and Their Standard Deviations

The sample standard deviation for the 1,600–1,799 cell—the appropriate cell for forecasting the selling price of your house—was $8,513, but was based on only four observations (and therefore three degrees of freedom). Does this properly measure our forecast uncertainty? Although the standard deviations for each cell are different, they are all based on very limited numbers of observations; could the differences have arisen by sampling error? Finally, it would be nice to have a measure of the overall efficacy of our partitioning the sample data into cells: have we really reduced the forecast uncertainty by this partitioning?

### Table 4.2

| HOUSE SELLING PRICE | HOUSE SIZE (SQ. FT.) |
|---|---|
| $109,360 | 1,404 |
| $137,980 | 1,477 |
| $131,230 | 1,503 |
| $130,230 | 1,552 |
| $125,410 | 1,608 |
| $124,370 | 1,633 |
| $139,030 | 1,717 |
| $140,160 | 1,775 |
| $144,220 | 1,832 |
| $154,190 | 1,934 |

### Table 4.3

| | ALL TEN HOUSES | SIZE RANGE (SQ. FT.) | | |
|---|---|---|---|---|
| | | 1,400 – 1,599 | 1,600 – 1,799 | 1,800 – 1,999 |
| Sample Average | $133,618 | $127,200 | $132,243 | $149,205 |
| Sample Standard Deviation | $12,406 | $12,381 | $8,513 | $7,050 |
| Number of Observations | 10 | 4 | 4 | 2 |

To shed light on these questions, we start by defining a **sample residual** as the difference between an actual value of the dependent variable and its estimated or forecast value. The first house in our sample belongs to the 1,400 – 1,599 cell. Its selling price was $109,360. The average selling price of the four houses in that cell was $127,200, and that was our point forecast for each of those four houses. The residual is then $109,360 – $127,200 = –17,840. We can calculate residuals for the remaining sample observations in the same way: for each observation, we identify its cell, use the cell average as a point forecast, and compute as its residual its actual selling price less the forecast. In Table 4.4 we show residuals computed in this way for the ten houses in your sample. (Negative numbers are shown in parentheses.) Notice that the mean of the residuals is zero.[3]

### Table 4.4

| | SELLING PRICE | RESIDUALS | SIZE | |
|---|---|---|---|---|
| | $109,360 | ($17,840) | 1,404 | |
| | $137,980 | $10,780 | 1,477 | Size = |
| | $131,230 | $4,030 | 1,503 | 1,400 – 1,599 |
| | $130,230 | $3,030 | 1,552 | |
| AVERAGE | $127,200 | | | |
| | $125,410 | ($6,833) | 1,608 | |
| | $124,370 | ($7,873) | 1,633 | Size = |
| | $139,030 | $6,788 | 1,717 | 1,600 – 1,799 |
| | $140,160 | $7,918 | 1,775 | |
| AVERAGE | $132,243 | | | |
| | $144,220 | ($4,985) | 1,832 | Size = |
| | $154,190 | $4,985 | 1,934 | 1,800 – 1,999 |
| AVERAGE | $149,205 | | | |
| AVERAGE: | | $0 | | |
| SUM OF SQUARES: | | 727,012,525 | | |
| DEGREES OF FREEDOM: | | 7 | | |
| RSD: | | $10,191 | | |

If you believe that size is the only distinguishing factor—that no other independent variables can explain the variability in the residuals—and that residuals are not likely to be larger in magnitude, on average, in one cell than they are in another, then the residuals are indistinguishable. The residual of –$17,840 computed for the first observation, which belonged to the first cell, is just as relevant a measure of our forecast error as residuals computed for observations in the other two cells. Even though the three cell means are different, we use all ten residuals to derive an overall estimate of forecast error. If the residuals were all close to zero, you would feel quite confident about your forecast; if they were widely dispersed, you would feel less confident.

---

[3] The mean of the residuals in any cell must be zero, since each residual is the difference between a value in a cell and the cell mean. As a result, the mean of the residuals across all cells must be zero.

There are two tricks in computing the standard deviation of the sample residuals. One is a simplification. To compute any standard deviation, you take each value, subtract the mean, and square the difference. Since the mean of the residuals is zero, you can just square the residuals. You then add them, obtaining a "sum of squares," divide by the degrees of freedom, and take the square root. The second trick is computing the degrees of freedom. Each sample mean "uses up" a degree of freedom. In the partitioned housing data, there are three sample means. Hence there are only 10–3=7 degrees of freedom. At the bottom of Table 4.4, the various steps in computing the residual standard deviation (RSD) are shown in detail. The RSD is $10,191, a modest improvement over the sample standard deviation of $12,406.

## Using the Data More Efficiently

If there were still other variables—age of house, lot size, neighborhood, etc.—that were related to selling price, we could in principle continue this process of partitioning our data into more narrowly defined cells. With our sample of ten houses, this is hardly feasible; with a very large sample, however, it would be practical to create "look-alike cells" that contained selling prices of houses that were alike with respect to several variables simultaneously. But, even with large samples, as the number of cells grows, the number of observations per cell and the degrees of freedom decline. On the one hand, a potential seller can identify a cell containing houses that look very much like her house; on the other hand, there will be very few such houses, and therefore her point estimate will be subject to large sampling error. And as the number of degrees of freedom declines, the denominator used in the calculation of the RSD gets smaller; although the numerator may also get smaller, the net effect may be for the RSD to increase—for your forecast uncertainty to get larger as you take into account more distinguishing factors.

In creating look-alike cells, we have used the data very inefficiently in two respects. First, we have ignored data on houses that are "almost like," but not "exactly like," yours. Wouldn't data about selling prices in the two size ranges adjacent to yours have some bearing on the selling price of your house? A second way in which we have used the data inefficiently is that we have partitioned it somewhat arbitrarily. Your house, with 1,682 square feet of living area, was treated as indistinguishable from houses of 1,600 or 1,799 square feet, but houses of 1,599 or 1,800 square feet were treated as irrelevant to your forecasting problem.

A way around both of these problems is to create a **model** that specifies the relationship between selling prices and the variables that help you forecast price—size, construction, lot size, age, etc. Selling price is the **dependent** variable; those variables that help you forecast price are the **explanatory** or **independent** variables.

# A REGRESSION MODEL

Let's first look at a model that relates selling price to size. While it is almost certainly true that some larger houses will sell for less than some smaller houses, it is reasonable to assume that as size goes up, selling price will go up **on average**. If each additional square foot increases average selling price by the same amount, the relationship between size and selling price is **linear**.

If each additional square foot increases selling price, but by less and less as size increases, the relationship is curvilinear, exhibiting **diminishing returns to scale**. If, on the contrary, each additional square foot increases selling price by a greater and greater amount, the relationship is again curvilinear, but this time exhibits **increasing returns to scale**. We can examine a scatter diagram to get clues about the relationship.[4]

Suppose we decide that the relationship is a linear one. We can express such a relationship as the following regression model:

$$y_{est} = b_0 + b_1 * x_1 ,$$

where $y_{est}$ is an estimate or point forecast of the actual selling price ($y$) of a house whose size (in square feet) is $x_1$, and $b_0$ and $b_1$ are constants (called **regression coefficients**) whose values are to be estimated from the data. Because we have assumed that the linear relationship between size and forecast selling price applies across all of the data, we can use all of the data to estimate the regression coefficients.

The regression coefficients are estimated by **least squares**. In principle, we could find the least-squares estimates by: (1) choosing arbitrary values of $b_0$ and $b_1$; (2) computing a forecast $y_{est}$ of each house's selling price by multiplying its size by $b_1$ and adding $b_0$; (3) computing a residual $y - y_{est}$ for each house (the difference between its actual and its forecast selling price); and (4) squaring and summing all the residuals. We would then select new values of $b_0$ and $b_1$ and go through the same four steps, finally choosing as our least-squares estimates the values of $b_0$ and $b_1$ for which the sum of squared residuals is least. This process could be easily extended to problems which contain more than one independent variable.

Fortunately, we don't have to go through this tedious sequence of steps. Just as the mean is a least-squares estimate of a single variable, so there are formulas for obtaining least-squares regression coefficients, but these formulas require so much computation that the only practical way of solving regression problems is with a computer.

Regression programs may differ in how data are entered and how the output is expressed, but they all have certain elements in common.

## INPUTS TO A REGRESSION ANALYSIS

You must supply the following information to the computer to perform a regression analysis:

1. *Identify the dependent variable.* The dependent variable is the variable that you want to forecast (selling price, in the example above).

2. *Specify the independent variable or variables.* The independent variables are those distinguishing factors that, in your judgment, help to explain the variation in the values of the dependent variable.

3. *Specify the relevant data.* Typically, your analysis will include all the data for which a specified relationship applies. Sometimes, however, it is hard to find a single relationship that links disparate groups of data. Suppose the house whose selling price we wanted to forecast were in Boston, and that our ten observations on house sales were for sales in Boston.

---

[4] How to detect and specify a curvilinear relationship, including increasing or diminishing returns to scale, is discussed later in this chapter.

If we could augment the data set to include houses in New York as well, we might find it difficult to specify a relationship between size and price that applied to both Boston and New York. We might choose to ignore the New York data, using only the Boston data to forecast Boston prices.

4. *Specify the nature of the relationship between the dependent variable and the independent variables.* This step requires some careful thought. As illustrated above, a forecast selling price based on the size of a house depends on the relationship you specify between size and price (such as linear, or with increasing or decreasing returns to scale). The issues involved in specifying such relationships are discussed in more detail later in this chapter.

5. *Provide values of the dependent and independent variables for the relevant observations.* You must provide these values to the computer in the form of a data file. In the forecasting problem, you would have to provide a file containing the selling price, size, and whatever other variables you deemed relevant for the ten houses in your sample.

# OUTPUTS FROM A REGRESSION ANALYSIS

The computer generates output from the input discussed above. In this chapter we discuss three types of output: regression coefficients, forecasts, and measures of goodness of fit.

## Regression Coefficients

We saw in the last section that a regression model is a formula that relates a forecast or estimate of the dependent variable to the value(s) of the independent variable(s). The formula involves constants, called regression coefficients, whose values are estimated from the data. When there is only one independent variable and the relationship between the independent and the dependent variable is linear, there are two regression coefficients, $b_0$ and $b_1$.

Suppose we had the sample of ten houses shown in Table 4.2, with data on their selling prices and size. We perform a regression with selling price as the dependent variable and size as the independent variable (in the following discussion we refer to this regression as Model 1) and discover that $b_0 = 35,524$ and $b_1 = 59.69$. How do we interpret these regression coefficients? The value of $b_1$ tells us that if our regression model is specified correctly, each additional square foot of living space adds an average of about \$60 to the value of a house. The "constant" term $b_0$ tells us that an average house with 0 square feet will sell for around \$35,500. This interpretation of $b_0$ may seem utterly nonsensical, but let's not get distracted for the moment.

With just one independent variable, it is easy to visualize what is happening. Figure 4.1 is a scatter diagram of selling price vs. area. The straight line through the plotted points represents the "least-squares" fit to the data. It intersects the vertical axis at about 35,000 (the value of $b_0$), and has a slope of about 60 (the value of $b_1$): the line goes up from about \$35,000 to about \$95,000 over a range of 1,000 on the horizontal axis, or about 60 per unit increase in the independent variable.

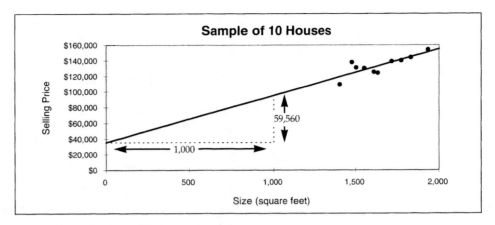

**Figure 4.1**

In any regression with just one independent variable ($x_1$), where the relationship between the dependent variable ($y$) and $x_1$ is assumed to be linear, least-squares estimates or forecasts $y_{est}$ as a function of $x_1$ can be graphed as a straight line (the regression line), with the equation

$$y_{est} = b_0 + b_1 x_1 .$$

In this equation, $b_0$ is the "intercept," the height of the regression line where it intersects the vertical axis, and $b_1$ is the slope, the amount the regression line increases per unit increase in $x_1$.

Now let's introduce a second independent variable: the age of the house (in years), symbolized by $x_2$, values of which are shown in the third column of Table 4.5. Let us specify as our regression model (Model 2)

$$y_{est} = b_0 + b_1 x_1 + b_2 x_2$$

where the values of $b_0$ and $b_1$ will be different from the values they had in Model 1. When we perform the regression, the least-squares estimates of the $b$'s are as follows: $b_0 = 4{,}045$, $b_1 = 86.84$, and $b_2 = -695.8$. (We summarize the results of Models 1 and 2 in Table 4.6.)

**Table 4.5**_____

| SELLING PRICE | SIZE (SQ.FT) | AGE |
|---|---|---|
| 109,360 | 1,404 | 20 |
| 137,980 | 1,477 | 2 |
| 131,230 | 1,503 | 5 |
| 130,230 | 1,552 | 4 |
| 125,410 | 1,608 | 23 |
| 124,370 | 1,633 | 34 |
| 139,030 | 1,717 | 25 |
| 140,160 | 1,775 | 23 |
| 144,220 | 1,832 | 28 |
| 154,190 | 1,934 | 25 |

**Table 4.6**_____

|  | MODEL 1 | MODEL 2 |
|---|---|---|
| CONSTANT TERM | 35,524 | 4,045 |
| COEFFICIENT FOR: |  |  |
| SIZE | 59.69 | 86.84 |
| AGE |  | (695.8) |

While it is much more difficult to visualize the relationship between $y_{est}$ and the $x$'s,[5] we can nevertheless interpret the $b$'s. The value of 4,045 for $b_0$ is the forecast price for a brand-new house with 0 square feet of living area. Although this estimate of the constant term is absurd, it is less so than the constant term of around 35,000 in Model 1. We'll have more to say about this later.

---

[5] We could depict the relationship by means of a three-dimensional graph. Such a graph is hard to visualize and doesn't get us very far: if we perform a regression with three or more independent variables there is no way of graphing the relationship.

The value of 86.84 for $b_1$ means that if $x_1$ increases by one unit (one square foot) while $x_2$ remains constant, $y_{est}$ will increase by 86.84: for houses of a given age, each additional square foot adds an average of $86.84 to their value. Notice that this is different from the regression coefficient of 59.69 associated with size in Model 1. We have learned one very important fact about regression: *the value of the regression coefficient associated with a given independent variable depends on what other independent variables are included in the model.*

Turning to the regression coefficient associated with age, we see that a one-unit increase in $x_2$, holding $x_1$ constant, *decreases* $y_{est}$ by 695.8: two houses of equal size that differ in age by one year will differ in price by nearly $700 on average; the older house will tend to be cheaper.

When a regression model involves two or more independent variables:

▶ the constant term is an estimate of the value of the dependent variable when all of the independent variables are equal to zero.

▶ the regression coefficient associated with a given independent variable is an estimate of the amount by which the dependent variable will change when the independent variable in question changes by one unit, while all the other independent variables *in the model* are held constant.

## Uncertainty in Regression Coefficients

The observations used in a regression analysis can almost always be thought of as a sample from some larger population or process; therefore the estimates derived from regression analysis are subject to sampling error. Just as the sample mean is an estimate of a population or process mean, so a regression based on sample data is an estimate of what the regression would be if we had in hand all the relevant data, not just a sample. In particular, each sample regression coefficient is a point estimate of a "true" regression coefficient. How much error there may be in this estimate is given by the regression coefficient's **standard error**. The formula for the standard error is fairly complicated, but virtually all computer programs compute and print its value.

In Chapter 2, "Sampling and Statistical Inference," we saw that the sample mean is an estimate of a population mean, and from this estimate and its standard error, you can derive a normal confidence distribution of the population mean, confidence intervals, and $t$ values. By analogy, the estimate and standard error of a regression coefficient enable you to derive a (normal) confidence distribution for the "true" regression coefficient, confidence intervals, and $t$ values.

In Model 1, the regression coefficient $b_1$ has an estimated value of 59.69 and a standard error of 15.10. With 68% confidence we can say that the "true" population coefficient is between 44.59 and 74.79, and 95% and 99.7% confidence intervals can be similarly constructed. The $t$ value is $59.69/15.10 = 3.95$. Since the value of $t$ exceeds 3, it is virtually certain that the "true" regression coefficient is positive.

In the same model, the constant term $b_0$ has an estimated value of 35,524 and a standard error of 24,933, implying a $t$ value of 1.42. It is certainly possible that the "true" value of the constant term is close to zero, or negative. The "nonsensical" estimated value of 35,524 may have arisen only as a result of sampling error.[6]

---

[6] Another reason that the constant term may be misleading derives from our assumption that size and selling price are linearly related. For sizes in the range observed in our sample, an assumption of linearity may be quite justifiable, but if we were to extrapolate in either direction far outside that range we might find the relationship to be curvilinear. In particular, if there are diminishing returns to scale, the intercept of an appropriate curve might be quite close to zero.

## Proxy Effects

We observed that $b_1$, the regression coefficient associated with size, had a value of 59.69 in Model 1 and a value of 86.84 in Model 2. Why are the values different? Recall that in Model 1 size was the only independent variable, whereas in Model 2 a second independent variable, age, was introduced. In Model 1, $b_1$ estimates the amount by which selling price increases when size increases by 1 square foot; in Model 2, it estimates the increase in selling price when size increases by 1 square foot *with age held constant*. Why is $b_1$ higher in this case? The argument is tricky, but let's take it step by step.

In Model 2 we saw that the relationship of age to selling price, when size is held constant, is negative ($b_2 = -695.8$): older houses tend to sell for less than newer houses of the same size. It also turns out that age and size are positively correlated; the correlation coefficient is 0.81. When age is left out of the regression, as in Model 1, size not only reflects its own relationship with selling price, but it also *proxies* for the relationship of age with selling price. Because the age-selling price relationship is negative, but age and size are positively correlated, the age effect for which size proxies is negative, and therefore $b_1$ turns out to be smaller than it was when the effect of age was held constant, as in Model 2.[7]

Proxy effects occur when two independent variables—say $x_1$ and $x_2$—(1) are correlated with each other; (2) are both related to the dependent variable ($y$), in the sense that both would have nonzero regression coefficients if both were included in the model; but (3) just one of them—say $x_1$—is included in a regression model, while the other is excluded. If all three of these conditions are satisfied, then $x_1$ will proxy for $x_2$, the proxy effect being greater the higher the correlation between $x_1$ and $x_2$ and the closer the relationship between $x_2$ and $y$. If both $x_1$ and $x_2$ are included in the model, their individual relationships with $y$ will be correctly sorted out, but there may be other independent variables that we failed to include in the model for which the included variables proxy.

Observe that *proxy effects have absolutely nothing to do with sampling error*. As you add variables to a regression model, the effect of these added variables on a particular regression coefficient may be positive or negative,[8] and *may* greatly exceed anything that could possibly be attributed to sampling error. On occasion, you will find that a regression coefficient that was positive in a one-independent-variable model turns negative as you add other independent variables, or vice versa.

---

[7] You can relate the results of Models 1 and 2 exactly as follows. Perform a regression with $x_2$ as the dependent variable and $x_1$ as the independent variable. Let $x_2$ (*est*) be the estimated value of $x_2$ derived from this regression; we find that

$$x_2 \ (est) = -45.24 + .03903x_1 \ .$$

Substituting this estimated value of $x_2$ for the actual value of $x_2$ in Model 2, we get

$$
\begin{aligned}
y_{es} &= 4{,}045 + 86.84x_1 - 695.8x_2 \\
&= 4{,}045 + 86.84x_1 - 695.8 \ (-45.24 + .03903x_1) \\
&= 4{,}045 + 86.84x_1 + 31{,}478 - 27.16x_1 \\
&= 35{,}523 + 59.68x_1
\end{aligned}
$$

which agrees with Model 1 except for a slight numerical rounding error.

[8] Whether the effect on a particular regression coefficient, say $b_1$, is positive or negative depends on (a) whether the added variable, say $x_2$, has a positive or negative regression coefficient in the model that includes it and $x_1$, and (b) whether the correlation between $x_1$ and $x_2$ is positive or negative.

## Two Common Misconceptions

Notice that in Model 2 the dependent variable was measured in dollars, and the two independent variables were measured in square feet and years, respectively. *It is often incorrectly assumed that variables used in a regression must be measured in comparable units.*

We also saw in Model 2 that the two independent variables, size and age, were correlated. *A common misconception is that variables used in a regression must be uncorrelated.*

# FORECASTS

## Point Forecasts

In any regression model, a point forecast of the dependent variable can be made by multiplying known values of the independent variables by their respective estimated regression coefficients, adding the products, and finally adding the estimated constant term. In Model 2, a point forecast for a house that has 1,682 square feet and is 10 years old is:

$$y_{est} = 4{,}045 + 86.84{*}1{,}682 - 695.8{*}10 = 143{,}152.$$

## Probabilistic Forecasts

When we perform a regression, we are attempting to take into account all distinguishing factors that can explain how a dependent variable varies in value. We only rarely can explain all such variation perfectly. What is left unexplained after a regression is performed is a collection of indistinguishable residuals—the differences between the actual values of the dependent variable $y$ and the corresponding point forecasts $y_{est}$. These residuals are retrospective, in the sense that they come from data already in hand. We want to forecast a prospective value of the dependent variable—a value not yet known. Our point forecast will almost surely be in error. We want to quantify and attach probabilities to these prospective errors.

We can link the variability of our retrospective residuals with the uncertainty in our prospective forecast errors by the following logic. Because the residuals are indistinguishable, any one is as representative of the error we are likely to make on a given forecast as any other. For many purposes it is sufficient to assume that each retrospective past residual corresponds to a prospective forecast error whose probability is equal to the relative frequency of the residual in question.

When a probabilistic forecast is to be used as an uncertainty in a decision problem, this method is quite satisfactory. Table 4.7, for example, shows the data on ten houses given in Table 4.5, plus estimated values and residuals based on Model 2. If we wanted to make a probabilistic forecast for your 1,682-square-foot 10-year-old house, we would start with the point forecast of $y_{est} = 143{,}152$. Each residual added to the point forecast would give a possible forecast value of $y$, and since there are ten residuals, each such value would be assigned probability 1/10. Figure 4.2 represents the uncertainty that we would assign to the selling price of your house based on the Model 2 regression results.

## Table 4.7

| SELLING PRICE | SIZE (SQ. FT.) | AGE | $y_{est} = 4{,}045 +$ $86.84*$SIZE$-$ $695.8*$AGE | RESIDUALS |
|---|---|---|---|---|
| 109,360 | 1,404 | 20 | 112,054 | (2,694) |
| 137,980 | 1,477 | 2 | 130,917 | 7,063 |
| 131,230 | 1,503 | 5 | 131,088 | 142 |
| 130,230 | 1,552 | 4 | 136,039 | (5,809) |
| 125,410 | 1,608 | 23 | 127,682 | (2,272) |
| 124,370 | 1,633 | 34 | 122,200 | 2,170 |
| 139,030 | 1,717 | 25 | 135,757 | 3,273 |
| 140,160 | 1,775 | 23 | 142,185 | (2,025) |
| 144,220 | 1,832 | 28 | 143,656 | 564 |
| 154,190 | 1,934 | 25 | 154,601 | (411) |

Sometimes you are not faced with a clearly defined decision, but a problem in which some uncertainty depends on your forecast. In this case you may want to reflect your forecast uncertainty in terms of confidence intervals. Standard practice is to *assume* that the sample residuals came from a population of normally distributed residuals, and thus to assume that the forecast errors are normally distributed, with mean zero and standard deviation equal to the estimated residual standard deviation, or RSD.[9] This in turn implies that the probability distribution for the forecast itself has mean $y_{est}$ and standard deviation equal to the RSD. For example, the RSD for the sample of ten houses is 4,072. Thus a 68% confidence interval for our 1,682-square-foot 10-year-old house is between $143{,}152 - 4{,}072 = 139{,}080$ and $143{,}152 + 4{,}072 = 147{,}224$.

| | | POINT FORECAST | RESIDUAL = FORECAST ERROR | PROBABILISTIC FORECAST |
|---|---|---|---|---|
| | 1/10 | 143,152 | (5,809) | 137,343 |
| | 1/10 | 143,152 | (2,694) | 140,458 |
| | 1/10 | 143,152 | (2,272) | 140,880 |
| | 1/10 | 143,152 | (2,025) | 141,127 |
| | 1/10 | 143,152 | (411) | 142,741 |
| | 1/10 | 143,152 | 142 | 143,294 |
| | 1/10 | 143,152 | 564 | 143,716 |
| | 1/10 | 143,152 | 2,170 | 145,322 |
| | 1/10 | 143,152 | 3,273 | 146,425 |
| | 1/10 | 143,152 | 7,063 | 150,215 |

*Figure 4.2*

---

[9] In a subsequent section, we show how to compute the regression RSD.

A schematic of how we go from a regression to a probabilistic forecast is shown in Figure 4.3.

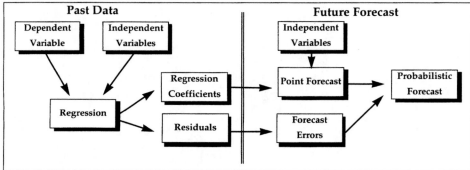

*Figure 4.3*

## Additional Sources of Uncertainty

Both methods of deriving probabilistic forecasts from a regression assume that the only source of uncertainty is the variability of the residuals. We have swept under the rug two other sources of uncertainty that are always present, and in practice there are often still other uncertainties. All of these uncertainties combine to make the true forecast distribution more dispersed than the distributions computed above. The 68% confidence interval computed in the last section should really have a lower limit less than 139,080 and an upper limit greater than 147,224.

Although we can correct mathematically for some sources of uncertainty, at the cost of greatly complicating the formulas for forecast distributions, some of the uncertainty depends on pure judgment. Rather than make a partial correction, we will treat all additional sources of uncertainty judgmentally.

We begin with uncertainties that are a result of sampling error. We know that the regression coefficients are only sample estimates of the "true" population regression coefficients. Residuals are computed as if these sample estimates are the true regression coefficients. Similarly, the sample RSD is only an estimate of the "true" variability of the "true" residuals in the population, but we use it as if it is a value known exactly.

We may encounter sources of uncertainty other than sampling error. For example, the independent variables used in a forecast are assumed to have known values, but in some situations they may be estimates or forecasts whose values are uncertain at the time that the forecast is made. And often the most important source of additional uncertainty is whether the independent variables used are truly relevant, and whether the representation of the relationship between the dependent and the independent variables is correct: a probabilistic forecast is made with respect to a particular regression model, but there are often a number of other plausible models that may lead to different forecasts.

Thus, in addition to the uncertainty attributable to the variability of the residuals—the only uncertainty embodied in the forecast distributions derived in the last section—there are, or may be, at least five other sources of uncertainty arising from:

▶ uncertainty in the values of the regression coefficients, whose estimated values we are treating as if they are known with certainty

▶ uncertainty in the RSD, whose estimated value we are treating as if it is known with certainty

- possible uncertainty in the values of the independent variables used in a forecast

- possible uncertainty about which one of several competing regression models is correct

- the assumption that the residuals come from a population of normally distributed residuals

It is very difficult to quantify the degree to which a forecast distribution computed in either of the two ways described above understates our uncertainty, but the problem is less severe if:

- there are many observations

- there are not many independent variables

- the values of the independent variables used in the forecast are well within the range of the independent variables in the data from which the regression model was constructed[10]

- the values of the independent variables used in the forecast are known with certainty[11]

- the regression model has no plausible competitors

- the model fits the data well

- the sample residuals are approximately normally distributed[12]

# Measures of Goodness of Fit

Regression programs provide various measures of goodness of fit, of which the two most important are the residual standard deviation (RSD) and the coefficient of determination, or $R^2$.

## Residual Standard Deviation

The residual standard deviation is just what it sounds like—the estimated standard deviation of the residuals—the square root of the sum of squared residuals[13] divided by the degrees of freedom. When we partitioned the data into "look-alike" cells, the degrees of freedom were the number of observations ($n$) less the number of cells. Here the degrees of freedom are $n$ minus the number of regression coefficients (including the constant term). Thus, in Model 2, there are $n = 10$ observations and three regression coefficients, so that there are seven degrees of freedom. The sum of squared residuals is 116,080,000, so that the RSD = $\sqrt{116,080,000 / 7}$ = 4,072.

---

[10] Extrapolating beyond the range of the data is dangerous for two reasons: (1) uncertainty in the regression coefficients becomes a more serious problem, and (2) a relationship between an independent and the dependent variable that appears to be linear over the range of data on which the regression was based may in fact be curvilinear; extrapolating a linear relationship in such a case can lead to serious errors.

[11] Independent variables that are "leading indicators" are especially useful in this respect: if next period's stock price, for example, depends on this period's inflation rate, one-period-ahead forecasts can be made using known values of the independent variable. Unfortunately, such leading indicators are not easy to find.

[12] A useful diagnostic tool is to plot a histogram of the sample residuals to see if the shape of the histogram is roughly normal.

[13] Just as was the case when we partitioned the sample into look-alike cells, residuals from any regression fitted by least squares necessarily have mean 0. Hence, in computing the standard deviation, we can add up the squared residuals without first subtracting out the mean.

In comparing regressions having the same observations and the same dependent variable, the one with a lower RSD indicates a better fit. As you add independent variables to a regression model, the sum of squared residuals almost always decreases (at worst, it doesn't change), but the degrees of freedom also decrease. Because both the numerator and the denominator tend to decrease as you add variables, the RSD may go in either direction. If adding a variable causes the RSD to increase, you almost surely have too many independent variables in your model.

## Coefficient of Determination ($R^2$)

While the RSD provides a good way of comparing different regression models in terms of goodness of fit, the measure is in units of the dependent variable, and it is hard to judge if an RSD of 4,072, say, indicates a good fit or a bad fit in an absolute sense. It is tempting to try to find an index that does not depend on the units of measurement of the variables in the regression. $R^2$ is such an index. As we shall see, however, it is a very fallible absolute measure of the goodness of fit.

$R^2$ measures the percent improvement in fit that a regression provides relative to a base case which assumes that the values of the dependent variable are indistinguishable. For the base case we compute the sum of squared residuals about the mean of the dependent variable; let's call this the "base-case sum of squares." If the sum of squared residuals from the regression—the "regression sum of squares"—is much less, the regression has explained much of the variability in the dependent variable, an indication of a good fit. If the regression sum of squares is almost as large as the base-case sum of squares, the regression has not explained much of the variability in the dependent variable: the fit is bad. $R^2$ measures the percent reduction in the base-case sum of squares achieved by the regression. Its formula is:

$$R^2 = (\text{base-case sum of squares} - \text{regression sum of squares})/\text{base-case sum of squares} .$$

In the housing data, the base-case sum of squares for selling prices is 1,385,300,000. We have already seen that the regression sum of squares is 116,080,000. Thus $R^2 = 0.9162$.

An alternative way of defining $R^2$ is as the square of the correlation between the values of $y_{est}$ and the true values ($y$) of the dependent variable. In the housing data, the correlation between the true selling price and the price estimated by Model 2 is 0.9572; its square is 0.9162.

Because the regression sum of squares will almost always decrease as you add independent variables, $R^2$ will always increase (or at worst remain unchanged) as you add variables. The computation of $R^2$ does not "penalize" you for using up degrees of freedom as you add variables.

## "Adjusted" $R^2$

Some regression programs provide an "adjusted" $R^2$ instead of, or in addition to, the ordinary $R^2$. Adjusted $R^2$ does take into account the degrees of freedom used up in by the regression. Specifically, instead of using the raw base-case and regression sums of squares, it first divides each by its respective degrees of freedom. Thus, in the housing example:

Adjusted $R^2 = (1,385,300,000/9 - 116,080,000/7)/(1,385,300,000/9) = 0.8923$ .

(The first term—1,385,300,000/9—is the square of the sample standard deviation of the dependent variable; the second is the square of the RSD.)

Adjusted $R^2$ is always less than ordinary $R^2$. It always increases when the RSD decreases and vice versa. As you add independent variables, it may or may not increase; if it decreases, that suggests you are using too many independent variables in your model. If you have few degrees of freedom and a poor fit, adjusted $R^2$ may be negative.

## Interpretation of $R^2$

Whether you use ordinary or adjusted $R^2$, you must remember that its interpretation is made relative to a base case that may itself be either a sensible way of forecasting the value of a future observation or a totally nonsensical way of forecasting. In the latter case, virtually *any* regression model is likely to produce a high value of $R^2$.

Here are a few benchmarks. You have data on the Standard and Poor's 500 stock index monthly closing price from January 1968 through March 1993. If you use time as an independent variable (January 1968 = 1, February 1968 = 2, etc.), $R^2 = 0.7586$; if you use last month's closing price as an independent variable, $R^2 = 0.9927$. You get high values of $R^2$ because the base case provides a nonsensical way of forecasting any particular month's S&P value: the "base-case" assumption that the values of the S&P 500 are indistinguishable over this twenty-five year period, when in fact they fluctuated between 63.54 and 451.67, had a pronounced upward trend, and a given month's price was generally much closer to the previous month's price than a price chosen at random, results in a base-case sum of squares which even the simplest regression models can reduce enormously.

Unfortunately, it does an investor very little good to forecast the *level* of the S&P 500. Investors make money by correctly forecasting *changes* in the level of a stock or an index. If you had a regression model for forecasting monthly changes in the S&P whose $R^2$ was only 0.05, you could, over the long run, do very well. Great value will accrue to an investor who can achieve even a small improvement over a base-case forecast that assumes that future changes will vary as past changes.

This should convince you that an $R^2$ of 0.99 does not necessarily indicate an extraordinary fit, nor does an $R^2$ of 0.05 mean that a regression is useless. It all depends on how difficult it is to do better than the base-case forecast.

# TRANSFORMED VARIABLES

Transformations greatly increase your ability to specify relationships between a dependent variable and a number of independent variables. In this section we shall show how transformed variables can be created that:

- permit independent variables to be used that are not contemporaneous with the dependent variable in a time series.
- permit you to use ordinal and categorical variables as independent variables.
- permit you to express relationships between a dependent and independent variable that are curvilinear.

## Lagged Variables in Time Series for Modeling Noncontemporaneous Effects

Suppose we believe that advertising affects sales. If we have a time series of a company's monthly advertising expenditures and unit sales, we could perform a regression with sales as the dependent and advertising as the independent variable, and see if there was any apparent relationship. Of course, we might want to include other variables, such as price, so that advertising does not inadvertently proxy for their effects.

On reflection, we might decide that although advertising this month might be related to sales this month, there might also be a carry-over effect from advertising expenditures made in previous months: last month's advertising might be related to this month's sales, and advertising expenditures two months ago might also have an influence, probably less, on this month's sales. We might believe that the effects of past advertising persist for some time.

Let $y_t$ be our unit sales in month $t$, $x_t$ be our advertising expenditure in the same month, and $p_t$ be our average selling price in month $t$. Then our original data would consist of values of $y_t$, $x_t$, and $p_t$ for as many months as we had data. To perform a regression in which sales depend on current and past values of advertising expenditure and current price, we would first compute **lagged transformations** $x_{t-1}$, $x_{t-2}$, etc., of $x_t$, and then run a regression with $y_t$ as the dependent variable, and $x_t$, $x_{t-1}$, $x_{t-2}$, $p_t$, and additional lagged $x$'s, if appropriate, as independent variables.

Values of lagged $x$'s are computed in Table 4.8 for hypothetical data. Notice that each time you lag a variable an additional period, you create a missing value (denoted by #N/A in the spreadsheet). Since an observation used in regression must be complete, i.e., no value missing for any variable used in the regression, lagging a variable results in lost observations. A regression with $x_t$, $x_{t-1}$, and $x_{t-2}$ as independent variables has four fewer degrees of freedom than one with just $x_t$ as an independent variable: two are lost because there are two more variables; two more are lost because there are two fewer observations.

### Table 4.8

| MONTH (t) | UNIT SALES (000) IN MONTH t | ADVERTISING EXPENDITURES ($000) IN MONTH t | ADVERTISING EXPENDITURES ($000) IN MONTH t−1 | ADVERTISING EXPENDITURES ($000) IN MONTH t−2 | AVERAGE UNIT PRICE IN MONTH t |
|---|---|---|---|---|---|
| Jan-92 | 1,137 | 1,144 | #N/A | #N/A | $6.57 |
| Feb-92 | 1,227 | 972 | 1,144 | #N/A | $6.95 |
| Mar-92 | 949 | 798 | 972 | 1,144 | $6.54 |
| Apr-92 | 842 | 861 | 798 | 972 | $6.53 |
| May-92 | 810 | 936 | 861 | 798 | $6.64 |
| Jun-92 | 707 | 770 | 936 | 861 | $6.21 |
| Jul-92 | 1,323 | 1,432 | 770 | 936 | $6.78 |
| Aug-92 | 1,471 | 1,330 | 1,432 | 770 | $6.91 |
| Sep-92 | 1,090 | 886 | 1,330 | 1,432 | $7.04 |
| Oct-92 | 890 | 996 | 886 | 1,330 | $7.90 |
| Nov-92 | 646 | 596 | 996 | 886 | $6.09 |
| Dec-92 | 757 | 774 | 596 | 996 | $6.23 |
| Jan-93 | 934 | 1,142 | 774 | 596 | $6.62 |
| Feb-93 | 1,071 | 932 | 1,142 | 774 | $6.39 |
| Mar-93 | 1,165 | 972 | 932 | 1,142 | $6.04 |

We can lag not only values of an independent variable, but also values of the dependent variable. We might believe that sales levels tend to persist: this month's level is more likely to be high if last month's was high than if last month's was low. In that case, we might include $y_{t-1}$ as an independent variable. If we believe that levels of sales in the more remote past tend to persist into the present, we could include values of $y_{t-2}$, $y_{t-3}$, etc. as independent variables as well. As before, each additional lag "costs" two degrees of freedom, one for the additional independent variable in the model, one for the observation lost in creating the lag.

## Dummy Variables for Modeling Effects of Ordinal or Categorical Variables

Sometimes ordinal or categorical variables may be plausible explanatory variables in a regression. Selling prices of houses might depend on their condition; suppose, for each of the houses in your sample, we had an indication of its condition, on a scale from 1 to 5, 1 indicating "poor" and 5 indicating "excellent." Everything else being equal, we would expect that as condition gets better, selling price goes up, on average. But how do we deal with an ordinal variable like this in regression? If $x$ represents the variable, and has possible values of 1 through 5, just including $x$ in the model implies that, everything else being equal, the average difference in selling price between two houses rated 1 and 2 ("poor" and "fair") will be the same as for two houses rated 4 and 5 ("good" and "excellent"). But because the variable is ordinal, the difference between ratings of 1 and 2 may not measure the same difference in condition as the difference between 4 and 5. If we really believe the differences may be substantial, just using the rating scale $x$ as an independent variable misspecifies the relationship between condition and selling price.

An even more serious problem occurs with categorical data. You might have a variable representing quality of construction, in one of three categories: frame, mixed frame and brick, and all brick. If we coded those categories 1, 2, and 3 respectively, could we just use the coded variable as an independent variable in our regression? Of course not! It might be the case that, all other things being equal, mixed frame and brick houses sell for more, on average, than either frame or all brick. Such a relationship could not possibly be revealed by including the coded variable in the regression.

Dummy variables provide a way of specifying ordinal and categorical relationships. Let's start with the simplest case, where there are just two categories (male vs. female, Republican vs. Democrat, yes vs. no, etc.). Suppose we code one of the categories 1 and the other 0; the actual assignment is arbitrary. In our housing example, suppose there were just two types of construction instead of three: frame houses (coded 0), and brick houses (coded 1). If we include this dummy variable as an independent variable in a regression, the corresponding regression coefficient tells us by how much brick houses differ from frame houses in selling price, on average, when the other independent variables included in the regression are held constant. A regression coefficient of 1,234, for example, implies that brick houses sell, on average, for $1,234 more than frame houses that are alike in all other respects measured by the other independent variables in the model. If the regression coefficient were (3,456), it would imply that brick houses sell for $3,456 less than frame houses.[14]

---

[14] Notice that this specification implies that whatever the average difference in price, it is the same for large houses as it is for small, the same for old houses as for new, etc. If you believe that the difference will be larger for large houses than for small houses, say, a different model specification is needed. However, we do not discuss such "interactive" relationships in this chapter.

Now let's return to the case where there are three categories of construction. We will create *two* dummy variables. One dummy will have value 1 if the house is mixed frame and brick, 0 if it is not (i.e., if it is *either* frame *or* all brick); the other will have value 1 if the house is all brick, 0 if it is not. In this specification, the third category—frame—will represent a "base case" as follows. Suppose the regression coefficients for the first and second dummies are 1,234 and (3,456) respectively. Remembering that we are talking about average relationships; with other variables included in the model held constant, these regression coefficients imply that, relative to the base case (frame houses), mixed frame and brick houses sell for $1,234 more, while all-brick houses sell for $3,456 less.

Suppose we had selected some other category—say all brick—as the base case. Then the regression coefficient for frame houses would be 3,456 and for mixed frame and brick 4,690 and we would reach the same conclusion as before: mixed frame and brick houses sell for $1,234 more, and frame houses for $3,456 more, than all brick. (The constant term would also change, decreasing by 3,456.) Although the choice of base case affects the values of the regression coefficients, it does not affect their interpretation.

In general, when a categorical or an ordinal variable has $c$ categories, you can represent the effect of each category by defining $c–1$ dummy variables, use any one of the categories as a base case, and then use the $c–1$ dummy variables, along with whatever other independent variables are appropriate, in the regression.

## Detecting, Specifying, and Interpreting Curvilinear Relationships: Exploratory Analysis

Suppose you suspect that in a model with more than one independent variable, the relationship between a particular independent variable ($x$) and the dependent variable ($y$) is curvilinear rather than linear. A scatter diagram of $x$ against $y$ might reveal such curvilinearity. But the relationship between $x$ and $y$ will be distorted by the proxy effects of the other independent variables on $x$.

A better way to detect curvilinearity under these circumstances would be to perform a regression using all the variables, compute the residuals, and plot the residuals (on the vertical axis) against $x$ (on the horizontal). If this plot looks curvilinear, it suggests that the relationship between $y$ and $x$, when all the other independent variables in the model are held constant, is curvilinear.

An even easier "quick and dirty" method of detecting curvilinearity is to include both $x$ and a squared transformation of $x$ (i.e., $x^2$), along with all the other independent variables, in the regression model. Thus, the model is specified as:

$$y_{est} = b_0 + a_1x + a_2x^2 + b_1x_1 + b_2x_2 + \ldots$$

where $x_1$, $x_2$, ... are the other independent variables and $a_1$ and $a_2$ are just the regression coefficients for $x$ and for $x^2$.

For fixed values of the other independent variables, a graph of $y_{est}$ as a function of $x$ will be a **parabola**, a curve that either rises to a peak and then descends, or that descends to a trough and then rises. A value of $a_2$ clearly different from 0 provides evidence of a curvilinear net relationship between $x$ and $y$; if, on the other hand, $a_2$ differs from 0 only by chance (sampling error), the data do not supply strong evidence of a curvilinear relationship.

Adding a squared transformation of an independent variable to the model thus provides an easy way of *detecting* curvilinearity, but *understanding* in what way the relationship between $y$ and $x$ is curvilinear is a trickier matter. To interpret the nature of the relationship correctly, two facts about parabolas are important to know:

1. If $a_2$ (the regression coefficient for $x^2$ in the previous equation) is *negative*, the parabola rises to a peak and then descends, while if $a_2$ is *positive*, the parabola first descends to a trough and then rises again.

2. The trough or peak occurs at the value of $x$ for which $x = -a_1/(2a_2)$.

The behavior of the estimate depends on whether $a_2$ is positive or negative, and whether all, or nearly all, of the values of $x$ are on one side or the other of the critical value $-a_1/(2a_2)$, or whether they substantially straddle that value. Table 4.9 shows six cases to consider:

**Table 4.9**

| CASE # | VALUES OF X | VALUE OF $a_2$ | BEHAVIOR OF $y_{est}$ |
|---|---|---|---|
| 1 | $x < -a_1/(2a_2)$ | $a_2 < 0$ | Increases at a decreasing rate (Decreasing returns to scale) |
| 2 | $x > -a_1/(2a_2)$ | $a_2 < 0$ | Decreases at an increasing rate |
| 3 | $x$ straddles $-a_1/(2a_2)$ | $a_2 < 0$ | Increases to max., then decreases |
| 4 | $x < -a_1/(2a_2)$ | $a_2 > 0$ | Decreases at a decreasing rate |
| 5 | $x > -a_1/(2a_2)$ | $a_2 > 0$ | Increases at an increasing rate (Increasing returns to scale) |
| 6 | $x$ straddles $-a_1/(2a_2)$ | $a_2 > 0$ | Decreases to min., then increases |

Figure 4.4 shows these cases. The arrows indicate the location of $-a_1/(2a_2)$ relative to the values of $x$ in the data.

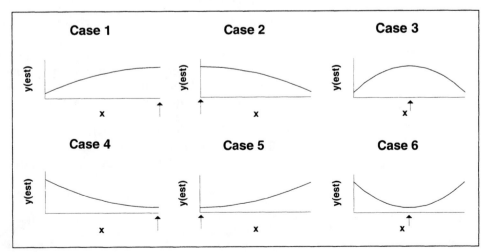

**Figure 4.4**

If, for example, $a_1 = 17.43$ and $a_2 = -2.367$, then $-a_1/(2a_2) = 3.682$ and if most of the values of $x$ are above 3.682, Case 2 applies: $y_{est}$ decreases at an increasing rate as $x$ increases.

This method of analysis, it should be repeated, is *exploratory*: it will usually reveal curvilinear relationships and permit you to classify them appropriately. Three points are worth making:

1. When introducing a squared transformation ($x^2$), be sure to include the original value of $x$ in the model as well.

2. The method discussed here will not reveal more complicated curvilinear behavior—for example, a relationship between $y$ and $x$ in which $y$ first increases at an increasing rate and then at a decreasing rate as $x$ increases.

3. Even if the general curvilinear relationship between $y$ and $x$ is detected and properly interpreted, the form of the model, using $x$ and $x^2$ to capture the curvilinearity, may be inappropriate. In particular, curvilinearity is often a consequence of a multiplicative relationship between $y$ and $x$, in which case modeling the relationship by using logarithmic transformations is appropriate. For details, see *Multiplicative Regression Models*, Chapter 6.

# USING THE REGRESSION UTILITY

The regression utility supplied with this text lets you perform regressions on data in Excel files, view various outputs, and make forecasts of values of the dependent variable when corresponding values of the independent variables are known. Although Excel has an "add-in" regression feature, the utility is being made available because it is easy to use.[15] This section provides instructions for using the utility, and then guides you through worked examples that show both how the utility is used and how to specify and interpret the results of regression analyses.

## Performing Regressions

### 1. Setting Up the Problem

*Opening the Data File.*    Use the File Open commands in Excel to open the relevant data file.

*Activating the Regression Utility.*    Follow the instructions distributed with the regression utility to activate it.

*Setting Up the Data Range.*    Highlight the entire block of data you want to analyze. This block of data should include all observations of the variables you want to analyze.[16] In addition, you may include (only) one row of column labels. Column/variable labels appear in the regression output and are a convenient way of describing data. If your labels extend over several rows, you may want to insert a new row with abbreviated labels just above the first row of data.

To select the data range, click on the column label of the cell in the upper-left corner of the block and highlight the entire block of data. To highlight a large database quickly hold down the [Shift] and [Ctrl] keys (on DOS computers), or the [Shift] and [Command][17] keys (on Macs), then

---

[15] The Excel add-in requires that all independent variables be in contiguous columns, which necessitates considerable shuffling of columns before each regression is run. Also, it has no facility for excluding observations, and its output is hard to interpret. The regression utility avoids these limitations.

[16] If you have created new transformations of variables in your data file, these transformations should be included in your data range. If you think you may create new transformations, you can reserve an appropriate number of columns by specifying a data range that extends to the right beyond the existing data. (Alternatively, you can create new, transformed variables and then respecify the data range.)

[17] Throughout this text, whenever the DOS control key is mentioned, Mac users should interpret it as the command key.

press first the down arrow and then the right arrow. This sequence highlights the block of data, unless there are missing observations that cause the highlighting to stop prematurely.

Choose **Data** from the menu bar and **Regression** from the pull-down menu, then **Set Data Range** from the Regression menu. When prompted, "Does the top row of your data range contain column (or variable) labels?," click **Yes** if in fact you have included the labels in your data range, as suggested earlier. When the process is complete, your data should be surrounded by a box.

### 2. Setting Up the Dependent Variable Column

Click any cell in the column you want to be your dependent variable. Again choose **Data** from the menu bar and **Regression** from the pull-down menu, then **Set dependent variable column** from the Regression menu. You should then see the values in the dependent variable column in bold type.[18]

### 3. Setting Up the Independent Variable Column(s)

Click any cell in the first column you want to select as an independent variable. If you want to select more than one independent variable and they are in *adjacent* columns, you can highlight any row containing the range of columns. If you want to select *nonadjacent* columns, hold down the [Ctrl] key as you click a cell in each column you want to select as an independent variable. Once you have selected all the columns containing independent variables, choose **Data** from the menu bar and **Regression** from the pull-down menu, then **Set independent variable column(s)** from the Regression menu. You should see the values in the independent variable columns with a shaded background.

### 4. Performing the Regression

Before initiating the regression calculations, you may need to exclude observations.

***Setting Up the Excluded Observations.*** The Regression utility will not calculate if you have observations with any values missing, so you will need to exclude observations containing such missing values. You may want to exclude observations for other reasons as well. If, after examining the data, you want to exclude observations from the database, hold down the [Ctrl] key and click a cell in each row you want to exclude. Choose **Data** from the menu bar and **Regression** from the pull-down menu, and choose **Set excluded observation(s)** from the Regression menu. Values of the variables in rows that were excluded will appear with strikeout lines through them.

***Performing the regression.*** Choose **Data** from the menu bar and **Regression** from the pull-down menu, then **Perform regression** from the Regression menu. The statistics will be calculated for you. Once the regression has been performed, you will find yourself in the rows below your database looking at the output.

## Outputs

A sample of the output that appears after you have chosen the **Perform regression** option is shown in Figure 4.5. This output was generated from the data set HTWT.XLS. Our model used weight as the dependent variable, and height and gender as the independent or explanatory variables.

---

[18] If you should happen to see "#####" signs, it means that your column width is too narrow. To widen the column, click on the letter of the column, select **Format** from the menu bar, **Column** from the pull-down menu, the **Autofit Selection** from the dialog box. Your column should now be wide enough to allow you to see the numbers.

**Figure 4.5**

| | **Regression Number 1** | | |
|---|---|---|---|
| | Dependent Variable: WT | | |
| | <u>HT</u> | <u>Constant</u> | <u>M/F</u> |
| Regr. Coef. | 4.198 | (133.7) | (17.86) |
| Std. Error | 0.210 | 14.9 | 1.74 |
| t value | 20.0 | (9.0) | (10.3) |

| | | | |
|---|---|---|---|
| # of obs = | **768** | Deg of F = | **765** |
| R-squared = | **0.6092** | Resid SD = | **15.94** |

The "constant" term will always appear in the dependent variable column.

### 5. Calculate $Y_{est}$ and Residual Values

Once you have looked at the regression statistics, you may want to calculate $Y_{est}$ (the regression estimates of the dependent variable) and residual values for the observations in your data range. This procedure can be time-consuming for large data sets. To initiate this process, choose **Data** from the menu bar and **Regression** from the pull-down menu, and **Calculate $Y_{est}$ and residual values** from the Regression menu. The values of $Y_{est}$ and the residuals appear in two columns to the right of the data range you selected.

### 6. View Charts

There are five different types of scatter diagrams to view. For charts involving $Y_{est}$ and/or residual values, you must of course calculate those values first, using the procedure described above. The charts available are:

$Y_{est}$ vs. $Y_{act}$ (the actual value of the dependent variable)
$Y_{est}$ vs. Residuals
Any $X$ vs. $Y_{act}$
Any $X$ vs. Residuals
Any $X$ vs. any other $X$

To view the charts, choose **Data** from the menu bar and **Regression** from the pull-down menu, and **View charts** from the Regression menu. Within the dialog box, click on the chart you want to view. To move to a second chart, just repeat the preceding steps.

## Forecasting

If you have a number of past observations on a dependent variable and a set of independent variables, and you want to forecast values of the dependent variable on future observations given specified values of the independent variables, do this:

1.  Be sure that the values of the *independent* variables on future observations are appended to the past observations in the data file.
2.  Leave the values of the *dependent* variable on these observations blank.
3.  Set the data range to include both the past and future observations.
4.  Set the dependent variable, then set the independent variables.
5.  Exclude the future observations, using the **Set excluded observation(s)** option from the Regression menu.
6.  Perform the regression.
7.  Calculate $Y_{est}$ and Residual Values.

The values of $Y_{est}$ on the future observations are point forecasts for those observations. (Because the future observations were excluded, values of all the variables on these observations, including $Y_{est}$, will appear with a strikeout line.) Residuals on the missing observations have values that are completely arbitrary; they may appear as blanks or with some error code, which you can safely ignore.

## Performing Another Regression

***Reset Current Settings.*** Once you have finished reviewing the output from your first regression, you may want to run a second regression. Choose **Data/ Regression,**[*] then **Reset current settings** from the Regression menu. Often you will want to keep the data range, but select different dependent and independent variables. Depending on what you want to change, you can then select the ranges to clear:

▶ Dependent variable column

▶ Independent variable columns

▶ Excluded observations

▶ Clear all ranges

Once you have cleared the ranges, set your new variables and perform the regression again. Your regression output will again appear below your data set, but *above* your first regression. It will be numbered Regression Number 2. Again, if you want to calculate values of $Y_{est}$ and residuals, or view charts requiring those columns, you will need to select those options again. Old values of $Y_{est}$ and residuals will be overwritten.

***Return to Prior Regressions.*** If you want to return to a prior regression, choose **Data/Regression**, then **Prior regressions** from the Regression menu. You will be prompted "Which one of your prior regressions would you like to retrieve?" Type in the number you want to retrieve. Keep in mind that you will need to choose **Calculate $Y_{est}$ and residual values** again if you want to look at charts for these data.

***View Statistics.*** This choice will allow you to move to the regression output portion of the spreadsheet. Just choose **Data/Regression** and then **View statistics** from the Regression menu.

***Print Statistics.*** This choice allows you to print the regression statistics. Choose **Data/Regression** and then **Print statistics** from the Regression menu.

# DOING REGRESSION ANALYSIS

We will now use the regression utility to analyze three data sets. You will learn how to perform a regression, understand regression output, diagnose violations of regression assumptions, transform variables, and make forecasts.

A good precursor to any regression analysis consists of doing the kinds of graphical analysis (scatter diagrams and time-series charts) discussed in Chapter 1. Many of these graphical analyses can be done within the regression utility.

## ▼ Example 1: Burlington Press

The Burlington Press publishes textbooks, primarily texts for junior high schools (seventh and eighth grade). As part of an analysis the company was carrying out in order to try to understand the market for their texts, the data in Figure 4.6 was collected on total purchases of texts for seventh grades by one city.

---

[*] This is shorthand for choose **Data** from the menu bar and **Regression** from the pull-down menu.

(The numbers give total purchases, not just Burlington's share.) Each seventh-grader received a set of texts from the school, used the books for the year, and then returned them. When new editions were brought out or when the schools conducted curriculum reviews, the texts for a particular subject might all be replaced at one time.

|   | A | B | C | D | E |
|---|---|---|---|---|---|
| 1 | | | | | |
| 2 | | | | | |
| 3 | | | | | |
| 4 | | | | Purchased | |
| 5 | | | Year | Texts | Students |
| 6 | | | 1967 | 2,111 | 2,000 |
| 7 | | | 1968 | 2,083 | 2,027 |
| 8 | | | 1969 | 2,264 | 2,050 |
| 9 | | | 1970 | 2,025 | 2,052 |
| 10 | | | 1971 | 2,303 | 2,061 |
| 11 | | | 1972 | 2,149 | 2,075 |
| 12 | | | 1973 | 2,177 | 2,079 |
| 13 | | | 1974 | 2,023 | 2,089 |
| 14 | | | 1975 | 2,178 | 2,091 |
| 15 | | | 1976 | 2,057 | 2,093 |
| 16 | | | 1977 | 2,371 | 2,131 |
| 17 | | | 1978 | 2,368 | 2,162 |
| 18 | | | 1979 | 2,439 | 2,194 |
| 19 | | | 1980 | 2,457 | 2,250 |
| 20 | | | 1981 | 2,764 | 2,292 |
| 21 | | | 1982 | 2,783 | 2,363 |
| 22 | | | 1983 | 2,596 | 2,412 |
| 23 | | | 1984 | 2,500 | 2,447 |
| 24 | | | 1985 | 2,598 | 2,470 |
| 25 | | | 1986 | 2,756 | 2,488 |
| 26 | | | 1987 | 2,457 | 2,502 |
| 27 | | | 1988 | 2,713 | 2,525 |
| 28 | | | 1989 | 2,748 | 2,567 |
| 29 | | | 1990 | 2,773 | 2,585 |
| 30 | | | | | |

**Figure 4.6**

How might you use this information to predict purchases of texts for the 1991 school year if the seventh-grade population (which was known quite closely six months before the start of school) was expected to be 2,600?

## Preliminary Analysis

**Data.** Burlington_Press is a worksheet in workbook REGRUTIL.XLS containing values of Year, Number of Purchased Texts, and Number of Students. The data in the file run from 1967 through 1990. A model for predicting purchases of texts might be:

$$Texts = B_0 + B_1*Year + B_2 * Students + error \qquad \text{(Model R1)} \ .$$

Since we want to forecast 1991 purchases, it is a good idea, before starting any analysis, to append a row to the data file consisting of what you know about 1991: the year and the number of students. Enter 1991 in the cell beneath "1990" (cell C31), and 2600 in cell E31. Leave cell D31, which represents the unknown Number of Purchased Texts for 1991, blank. The observation in row 31 is incomplete; we must remember to exclude it when we run the regression.

***Dependent and Independent Variables.*** Clearly, we are interested in forecasting Number of Purchased Texts; this is, therefore, the *dependent variable*. We might initially believe that the Number of Purchased Texts will increase or decrease with time, with number of students, or both. As a preliminary step, motivated especially to activate the graphics capabilities of the regression utility, let's designate School Year and Number of Students as *independent variables*.

***Running the Regression Utility.*** First, open REGRUTIL.XLS, and click on the Burlington_Press tab, and activate the regression utility. Now, click the label for the first data column **(C6)**. (Remember, we can use only one row of the column label.) To highlight the whole block of data, hold down the Shift and Control keys, then press [ **↓** ], then [ **→** ].

Click **Data/Regression** and then **Set data range**. Reply **"Yes"** to the next question; row 6 contains variable/column labels. Indicate the column containing the dependent variable by clicking any value in column D (Purchased Texts), then clicking **Data/Regression**, and on the **Set dependent variable column** from the Regression menu. The numbers in column D should now appear in boldface.

To indicate the columns containing the independent variables, click on any value in column C (School Year). Then while holding down [Ctrl] the move to any value in column E (Students) and click on that value. Both cells should be emphasized. Now click on **Data/Regression** and then on the **Set independent variable column(s)** option. The numbers in columns C and E should now appear with a shaded background.

The final step before performing the regression is to indicate the observation whose value is to be excluded. Move the cursor to row 31 (the observation for 1991), click any value in that row, click **Data/Regression**; then click the **Set excluded observation(s)** option. Row 31 now appears with strike-out bars through the numbers.

You have now told the regression utility everything it has to know; once again, click **Data/Regression** and then click **Perform regression**. After a moment you will see the regression output.

***Charts.*** Before trying to understand the regression output, let's look at what graphics capabilities are now available. Click **Data/Regression** and then click **View charts**. A dialogue box appears, giving you options for the five different kinds of charts discussed above:

- $Y_{est}$ vs. $Y_{act}$
- $Y_{est}$ vs. Residuals
- Any $X$ vs. $Y_{act}$
- Any $X$ vs. Residuals
- Any $X$ vs. any other $X$

As the values of $Y_{est}$ and residuals have not yet been computed, only the third and fifth options are available at this stage. If you take the third option, you can, for example, look at a time-series chart of Year vs. Number of Purchased Texts, or a scatter diagram of Number of Students vs. Number of Purchased Texts. If you take the fifth option, you can look at a time-series chart of Year vs. Number of Students. After you examine these charts, you can print any "current chart" by clicking **File** and then clicking the **Print** option.

***Computing $Y_{est}$, Residuals, and a Point Forecast.***   Click **Data/Regression** again, then click the **Calculate $Y_{est}$** and **residual values** option. After a short time two new columns (F and G) will be filled in with values of $Y_{est}$ and residuals. Compare the values of $Y_{est}$ with the values of Texts, year by year. They should be close. The difference between Texts purchased and $Y_{est}$ is the residual. If the regression estimated values of the dependent variable perfectly, all values of $Y_{est}$ would match the corresponding values of $Y$, and the residuals would all be zero.

Scroll down to row 31, the incomplete observation for 1991. You will see a value of 2,814 (displayed with a strikeout line) in column F. Given the regression model implied by the choice of dependent and independent variables (Model R1), this is the point forecast for the number of texts to be purchased in 1991.

## Regression Output

Let's turn now to the regression output. You can scroll to it, or click **Data/Regression** and then click the **View statistics** option. You will see lines of output labeled "Regr. Coef.," "Std. Error," and "t value." Below these are four other numbers, identified as "*# of obs*," "*Deg of F*," "*R-squared*," and "*Resid SD*." The output is shown in Table 4.10.

**Table 4.10**

**Regression Number 1**
Dependent Variable: TEXTS

|  | Year | Constant | Students |
|---|---|---|---|
| Regr. Coef. | 8.128 | (15,664) | 0.8824 |
| Std. Error | 16.454 | 31,289 | 0.5803 |
| t value | 0.5 | (0.5) | 1.5 |

| | | | |
|---|---|---|---|
| # of obs = | **24** | Deg of F = | **21** |
| R-squared = | **0.7638** | Resid SD = | **135.6** |

***Regression Coefficients.***   The numbers in columns C and E ("Year," and "Students") are associated with the independent variables. The numbers in column D are associated with the "constant term" in the regression equation; these constant-term values will always appear in the dependent-variable column, which simply is a convenient location in which to display them.

To interpret the first three lines of output, we must start with the realization that the regression that we performed assumed that the 24 observations in the data file were generated by a model of the form:

$$Texts = B_0 + B_1*Year + B_2 * Students + error, \qquad \text{(Model R1)}$$

where the $B$'s are constant but unobservable regression coefficients. From our sample of 24 observations, estimated values of the $B$'s (denoted by lower-case $b$'s) are obtained: $b_0 = (15,664)$, $b_1 = 8.128$, and $b_2 = 0.8824$. Given these estimated regression coefficients, you should verify that the values of $Texts_{est}$ can be computed by the formula:

$$Texts_{est} = -15,664 + 8.128*Year + 0.8824*Students \quad .$$

For example, the value[19] of $Texts_{est}$ for 1967 is:

$$Texts_{est} = -15{,}664 + 8.128*1967 + 0.8824*2{,}000 = 2{,}089$$

and the forecast for 1991 is:

$$Texts_{est} = -15{,}664 + 8.128*1991 + 0.8824*2{,}600 = 2{,}813 \quad .$$

Similarly, the values of the residuals can be computed from the formula:

$$Residuals = Texts - Texts_{est} \quad .$$

For example, the value of the residual for 1967 is:

$$Residual = 2{,}111 - 2{,}089 = 22 \quad .$$

You can add the 24 residuals in column G, using the =SUM function, and verify that their sum is 0.[20] If, in column H, you compute the values of the squared residuals and add them, you will find that they add to 386,276.3. If the estimated regression coefficients had any other values than the ones displayed, this sum would be higher; in that sense, the coefficients are estimated by **least squares.**

The estimated regression coefficients are derived from a sample and are therefore subject to sampling error. The next two lines of output—the Standard Error and the *t* value—provide information about sampling error similar in nature to the information that was provided in Chapter 2 for evaluating sampling error associated with estimates of a population mean. Thus the estimated value of the regression coefficient for Year, 8.128, is our best estimate of the increase in the Number of Texts Purchased from one year to the next, given that the Number of Students remains constant. That number is very uncertain, however. Using the standard error to construct confidence limits, we can say, for example, that, with 68% confidence, the true value of the regression coefficient lies between –8.326 and 24.582. To some degree, this uncertainty is reflected in the low *t* value of 0.5. Therefore, we cannot be at all confident that the sign of the true regression coefficient is positive: from the data alone, it is far from certain that the number of texts purchased will increase over time unless the number of students increases.

***Observations and Degrees of Freedom.*** Turning to the last four outputs, there were 24 observations used to estimate the two regression coefficients and the constant term; since three estimates were generated from the data, this leaves only $24 - 3 = 21$ degrees of freedom.

***Residual Standard Deviation.*** The residual standard deviation (often abbreviated as RSD) of 135.6 is an estimate of the standard deviation of the errors. It is computed as the standard deviation of the residuals in column G, "corrected for degrees of freedom." We have already observed that the sum of squared residuals is 386,276.3, and since the mean of the residuals is zero, this sum is also the sum of squared deviations from the mean. If we divide this sum by the number of degrees of freedom, 21, and take the square root, we get 135.6, the value given in the regression output.

---

[19] These numbers all happen to differ by 1 from the numbers printed for $Y_{est}$ and the residuals by the regression utility. This is because of roundoff error. If you compute the numbers in Excel, pointing to the cells containing the values of the estimated regression coefficients, you will get numbers that agree with the values of $Y_{est}$ and the residuals displayed by the utility.

[20] You may actually see a number like 8.6402E-12, which is "scientific notation" for 0.0000000000086402, which, accounting for roundoff error, is essentially zero.

***R-squared (R²).***     Finally, R-squared (or $R^2$) is computed by taking the square of the ratio of two standard deviations. The numerator of the ratio is the standard deviation of $Y_{est}$; the denominator is the standard deviation of $Y$.

Use the =STDEVP function to compute the standard deviation of $Y_{est}$ in cells F7 through F30; you should get 228.16. Now do the same for the values of $Y$ in cells D7 through D30; the standard deviation is 261.06. Finally, compute $(228.16/261.06)^2 = 0.7638$, the value of $R^2$ reported in the regression output (Table 4.10). If $Y_{est}$ perfectly predicts $Y$ on all observations, then $Y_{est}$ and $Y$ will have identical standard deviations and $R^2 = 1$. If the regression has absolutely no predictive power, the values of $Y_{est}$ will be the same on every observation: they will have values equal to the mean of $Y$, and their standard deviation will be 0. Thus in this latter case, $R^2 = 0$.[21]

Alternatively, $R^2$ can be computed as the square of the coefficient of correlation between $Y$ and $Y_{est}$. If $Y_{est}$ is a very good predictor of $Y$, then the two will be highly correlated and $R^2$ will be near 1. If the independent variables have no predictive power in relation to the dependent variable, then $Y_{est}$ will be a poor predictor of $Y$, and their correlation will be near 0, as will $R^2$. The first chart available under the **View charts** option plots a scatter diagram of $Y_{est}$ vs. $Y$. It provides a graphical view of the goodness of fit of the regression, which is summarized numerically by $R^2$.

In comparing competing regression models having the same dependent variable, a model with higher $R^2$ and lower RSD certainly indicates a better fit, and may indicate a better model, although it is certainly possible, by "fishing" through the data, to find independent variables that have no apparent relationship to the dependent variable but by chance are correlated with it in the data. Adding an independent variable, no matter how unrelated to the dependent variable, will never cause $R^2$ to decrease, but because the RSD is "corrected for degrees of freedom" and one more variable uses up one more degree of freedom, the RSD *may* increase. When the RSD increases when you add a new variable, you usually have evidence of "overfitting."

Except for the problem of overfitting, $R^2$ is a reasonable measure for comparing competing regression models, but just what constitutes a "good" $R^2$ depends on judgment. You should remember that the base case against which goodness of fit is measured is just using the mean of the dependent variable as an estimate of its value on all observations. In data with an upward trend, such as many economic time series have, this base-case measure is absurdly naive; any simple model which did no more than recognize the trend would do substantially better. Because it is so easy, when there is a pronounced trend, to do better than the base-case forecast, you should not be surprised to have a high value of $R^2$, nor should you conclude from the fact that $R^2$ is high that your model is necessarily a good one. If, on the other hand, you had a model that could predict daily change in stock prices that, without overfitting, had an $R^2$ of just 0.05, you could become very rich very quickly.

## Transformations

We turn now to a discussion of transformations, one of the ways in which you can add flexibility to how you specify a model, and one of the useful tools for converting a model which violates some of the regression assumptions to one that conforms more closely to those assumptions.

---

[21] Statisticians call the square of the standard deviation the variance. Thus $R^2$ is the ratio of two variances, with that of $Y_{est}$ in the numerator and $Y$ in the denominator. For this reason, $R^2$ is sometimes defined as the fraction of the variance of $Y$ that is "explained" by the regression.

Returning to the Burlington Press, you might notice, either by scanning column G or by producing a chart showing a time series of the residuals, that the values of the residuals from 1977 through 1983 were all positive, and that this coincided with a period when the number of students was increasing relatively fast. Reflecting on the process by which texts are purchased, you might conclude that the number of sets of books that the school system will own at the end of any school year will be equal to the number of students that year;[22] that one or more books in a set may be replaced at the end of the year because individual books were damaged or lost, or because a new textbook was adopted for the entire class; and that complete sets must be purchased for whatever increase in the number of students occurs between the end of one year and the beginning of the next. We have no information on replacement of individual texts or adoption of new texts, but we now have reason to believe that two of the drivers of text purchases are:

▶ students last year

▶ additional students this year

These variables are not in the original data file, but they can be derived from variables that *are* in the original file. In regression parlance, such derived variables are called **transformations**. In a time series, a transformation that creates a variable whose values are those of some other variable in a prior period is called a **lag** transformation. One that creates a new variable that represents the change in the value of some other variable over some period of time is called a **difference** transformation. Thus the variable Students Last Year is derived by **lagging** Students This Year by one year; the variable Additional Students is derived as the difference between Students This Year and Students Last Year.

To create these variables in Excel, first start with a clean slate by clicking on **Data/Regression**, then on the option **Reset current settings**, and then on **Clear all ranges** when the dialog box appears. We will create the lagged variable Students Last Year in column F, and the difference variable New Students in column G. Enter column labels of "Last Year" and "New Students" in cells F6 and G6, respectively. Next, click on cell **F8** and set the value in that cell equal to the number of students in the preceding year; i.e., enter the formula = E7. The cell should now contain the value 2,000, the number of students in 1967. Now click on cell **G8** and set the value in that cell equal to the change in the number of students between 1967 and 1968, i.e., enter the formula = E8 − F8. The cell should contain the value 27.

Now copy cells F8 and G8 down as far as the data go (from row 9 to row 31).

***Regression Using Transformed Variables.*** We are now ready to run a new regression. The only trick is that in addition to excluding row 31 (the forecast), you must now exclude row 7 (the data for 1967, which is incomplete because we have no values for the newly created variables.) Before invoking the **Set excluded observation(s)** option, click on any value in row 7, scroll down to row 31 and, while holding down [Ctrl], click on any value in that row. To run the regression, you need to:

1. **Set Data range** (C6:G31)

2. **Set Dependent variable column** (column D)

3. **Set Independent variable column**(s) (columns F and G)

4. **Set Excluded observation(s)** (rows 7 and 31)

5. **Perform regression**

---

[22] There might be more sets than students in a year where enrollment declined, but declining enrollment has not occurred in the data in hand.

The model we are estimating can be formally stated as:

$$Texts = B_0 + B_1*\text{Students Last Year} + B_2*\text{New Students} + error$$

(Model R2)

The regression output is shown in Table 4.11. What does it imply? First, comparing it with the output of Regression 1, shown in Table 4.10,

- the value of $R^2$ is higher (0.8479 vs. 0.7638),
- the RSD is lower (108.4 vs. 135.6), and
- the $t$ values associated with the independent variables are much higher.

**Table 4.11**

**Regression Number 2**
Dependent Variable: TEXTS

|  | Constant | Last Year | New Students |
|---|---|---|---|
| Regr. Coef. | 51.80 | 0.9905 | 5.910 |
| Std. Error | 274.75 | 0.1259 | 1.311 |
| t value | 0.2 | 7.9 | 4.5 |

| | | | |
|---|---|---|---|
| # of obs = | **23** | Deg of F = | **20** |
| R-squared = | **0.8479** | Resid SD = | **108.4** |

On the other hand, because we have incomplete data for 1967, there is one less observation, and hence one less degree of freedom. Also, the $t$ value for the constant term suggests that the true value of the constant could easily be zero or negative, even though its sample value is positive. Nevertheless, the regression appears to fit the data much better than Regression 1, and it tells a simple story: on average, about one text is added to each set left by students last year, and new students acquire roughly six new texts; these two factors account for much of the variability in the number of texts purchased.

***Can We Do Better?***   Before making a forecast, we might ask whether we should have included Year as one of the independent variables in Regression 2. We can easily add a variable by clicking on the columns for Year, Students Last Year, and New Students, invoking the **Set independent variable column(s)** option, and performing the regression. The model we are now estimating is:

$$Texts = B_0 + B_1*\text{Year} + B_2*\text{Students Last Year} + B_3*\text{New Students} + error.$$

(Model R3)

The results of Regression 3 are shown in Table 4.12. Compared with Table 4.11 (Regression 2):

- $R^2$ has increased very slightly (from 0.8479 to 0.8496);
- RSD has increased (from 108.4 to 110.6);
- because one more independent variable was included, the degrees of freedom decreased (from 20 to 19);
- the $t$ values associated with the independent variables are much lower.

We can conclude that including Year as an independent variable has resulted in overfitting.

## Table 4.12 _____

**Regression Number 3**
Dependent Variable: TEXTS

|  | Year | Constant |  | Last Year | New Students |
|---|---|---|---|---|---|
| Regr. Coef. | 6.760 | (12,818) |  | 0.7664 | 5.654 |
| Std. Error | 14.513 | 27,633 |  | 0.4980 | 1.446 |
| t value | 0.5 | (0.5) |  | 1.5 | 3.9 |

|  |  |  |  |
|---|---|---|---|
| # of obs = | **23** | Deg of F = | **19** |
| R-squared = | **0.8496** | Resid SD = | **110.6** |

_____

***The Forecast.*** Return to Regression 2 by invoking the **Prior regressions** option, and compute $Y_{est}$ and the residuals, getting a point forecast of 2,701 for 1991; the confidence distribution for the forecast thus has mean 2,701 and standard deviation equal to the RSD, or 108.4. Assuming the residuals are normally distributed with mean given by $Y_{est}$ and standard deviation equal to the RSD, we can state with 95% confidence that texts purchased in 1991 will be approximately between $2,701 - 2*108.4$ and $2,701 + 2*108.4$, (between 2,484 and 2,918). In practice, however, the interval should be made somewhat wider to account for uncertainties that we have not included in these calculations.[23]

## ▼ Dummy Variables

Dummy variables have just two possible values, 0 and 1 (see Chapter 1). They can be used to code any two-valued variable: men vs. women, Republicans vs. Democrats, buyers vs. nonbuyers, etc. Dummy variables are often used as independent variables in a regression analysis.

## Example 2: HBS Students' Height, Weight and Gender

HTWT.XLS contains data on the heights (in inches) and weights (in pounds) of 597 men and 171 women (as reported by them) in a recent MBA class at Harvard Business School. In addition to the variables Height and Weight, the variable Gender, having value 1 if the person is a woman, 0 if a man, is included in the file.

Suppose we want to predict weight from height using the model:

$$WT = B_0 + B_1*HT + error \quad . \qquad \text{(Model R4)}$$

Table 4.13 shows the results of a regression with weight as the dependent and height as the independent variable. Based on the regression output, we would forecast the weight of a person 70 inches tall as:

$$WT_{est} = -228.9 + 5.510*70 = 156.8 \quad .$$

---

[23] Sources of additional uncertainty come from: (1) using estimated (as opposed to true) B's, (2) inferring the residual standard deviation from a sample of residuals instead of from the true process that generated the residuals, (3) possible uncertainty about the values of the $x$'s used in a forecast (are we sure that the number of students next year will be 2,600?), and (4) the possibility that the model is not correctly specified.

## Table 4.13 _____

**Regression Number 1**
Dependent Variable: WT

|  | HT | Constant |
|---|---|---|
| Regr. Coef. | 5.510 | (228.9) |
| Std. Error | 0.178 | 12.4 |
| t value | 30.9 | (18.5) |

|  |  |  |  |
|---|---|---|---|
| # of obs = | **768** | Deg of F = | **766** |
| R-squared = | **0.5554** | Resid SD = | **16.99** |

Table 4.14 shows similar regression output when both height and gender (M/F) are included as independent variables using the model:

$$WT = B_0 + B_1*HT + B_2*M/F + error \quad . \qquad \text{(Model R5)}$$

## Table 4.14 _____

**Regression Number 2**
Dependent Variable: WT

|  | HT | Constant | M/F |
|---|---|---|---|
| Regr. Coef. | 4.198 | (133.7) | (17.86) |
| Std. Error | 0.210 | 14.9 | 1.74 |
| t value | 20.0 | (9.0) | (10.3) |

|  |  |  |  |
|---|---|---|---|
| # of obs = | **768** | Deg of F = | **765** |
| R-squared = | **0.6092** | Resid SD = | **15.94** |

According to the output in Table 4.14, based on model R5, we would forecast the weight of a person 70 inches tall as:

$$WT_{est} = -133.7 + 4.198*70 - 17.86*0 = 160.2$$

pounds if the person were male, and as:

$$WT_{est} = -133.7 + 4.198*70 - 17.86*1 = 142.3$$

pounds if the person were female. Thus, women are forecast to be 17.9 pounds lighter than men of the same height, −17.9 being the regression coefficient associated with the dummy variable indicating gender. A comparison of Tables 4.13 and 4.14 clearly indicates that the regression that includes the dummy variable fits the data better and provides a more plausible model.[24]

We noted in Chapter 1 that one of the observations in the data file might be an outlier. If you compute the values of $Y_{est}$ and the residuals associated with Regression 2, and then plot $WT_{est}$ against the residuals using the **View Charts** option, (see Figure 4.7) you will notice one very negative residual, and if you now scroll through the data file, you will find a residual of −109 on line 577, associated with an observation for which a male student 72 inches tall claimed to weigh 60 pounds. This was obviously misreported or misrecorded, and should clearly be eliminated, using the **Set excluded observation(s)** option. After doing so, and rerunning the regression, we get the output shown in Table 4.15 (based on the Regression 5 model) that is a decided improvement in fit.

---

[24] Of course, both models have negative constant terms, implying that a sufficiently short person will have negative weight! This is merely an instance showing the dangers of extrapolating too far beyond the range of the data. If we had data that included infants, young children, and adults, we would almost surely find that the relationship between height and weight was curvilinear, and that the variability in weights was considerably higher at the tall end of the spectrum. Transformations of the variables would be required.

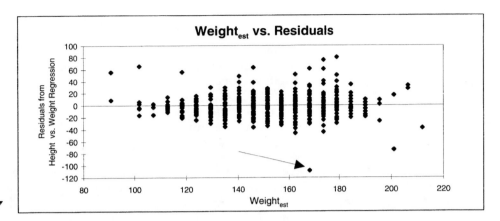

**Figure 4.7**

**Table 4.15**

**Regression Number 3**
Dependent Variable: WT

|  | HT | Constant | M/F |
|---|---|---|---|
| Regr. Coef. | 4.224 | (135.3) | (17.92) |
| Std. Error | 0.204 | 14.4 | 1.69 |
| t value | 20.7 | (9.4) | (10.6) |

| | | | |
|---|---|---|---|
| # of obs = | **767** | Deg of F = | **764** |
| R-squared = | **0.6263** | Resid SD = | **15.46** |

## ▼ Categorical Independent Variables

Often we have independent variables that are **categorical** (see Chapter 1). Individuals' political-party preference might be recorded as Republican, Democratic, or Independent, with codes of 1, 2, and 3 assigned arbitrarily to the three categories; companies may be classified by SIC codes; items sold by a retailer may be characterized by color, coded in some systematic but arbitrary manner. Using these variables directly in a regression clearly makes no sense.

Standard practice is to convert each possible value of a categorical variable into a dummy variable. Thus, in the political-party preference case, we would create a dummy variable that had the value 1 if the person was a Republican, and 0 if not; another dummy variable having the value 1 if a Democrat, 0 if not; and a third dummy variable similarly representing an Independent. In a regression, party preference would be taken into account by using two of these three dummy variables, omitting the third. Any two will do. The reason for using one less than the number of possible values of the categorical variable, and interpretations of the output, will be made clearer by introducing an example.

## Example 3: Brighton Catering Company

The president of the Brighton Catering Company was attempting to analyze data on labor costs of meals that the firm had prepared and served. Brighton's standard dinner included an appetizer, a main course, and a dessert. Customers could choose any one of three appetizers (fruit cocktail, shrimp cocktail, or melon with prosciutto). The firm also offered other options.

Customers might add a salad course, and they might include after-dinner drinks. The president wanted to adjust the firm's prices and, as a first step, wanted to understand the labor costs for different combinations of options. (Food costs would be considered separately.) Accordingly, careful cost studies had been conducted to determine the per guest labor costs of 35 different meals (with 100 to 150 guests each).

How could regression analysis be used to help predict the labor costs of a meal with shrimp cocktails, salad, and liqueurs? The data are in worksheet Brighton__Catering in workbook REGRUTIL.XLS. "Salad" and "Liqueurs" are each coded 1 if the item in question was served, 0 otherwise. "Appetizer" is coded 1 for Shrimp, 2 for Fruit Salad, and 3 for Melon and Prosciutto. We need to create a set of new variables to indicate whether a specific appetizer was served; we need to transform our categorical variable into three dummy variables, one for each category. In column G code 1 if Fruit was served, 0 otherwise (that is, if either Shrimp or Melon was served), and code the entries in columns H and I similarly for Shrimp and Melon.[25]

At the bottom of our data we entered values of the independent variables for three meals whose costs are to be forecast. In all three cases, a salad will be served, but not liqueurs, but the three cases differ with respect to appetizer.

In Table 4.16 we show the results of three regressions. In all three, Cost/Person is the dependent variable, and the three observations representing forecasts to be made are excluded. In the first regression, Salad, Liqueurs, and the first two of the Appetizer dummy variables—Fruit and Shrimp— are specified as independent variables. In the second regression, everything is the same except the last two of the Appetizer dummy variables—Shrimp and Melon—are specified, while in the third regression all three Appetizer dummies are used. Formally, the models can be stated:[26]

**Regression 1:**

$$COST = B_0 + B_1*SALAD + B_2*LIQUEURS + B_3*FRUIT$$
$$+ B_4*SHRIMP + error \quad , \qquad \text{(Model R7)}$$

**Regression 2:**

$$COST = B_0 + B_1*SALAD + B_2*LIQUEURS + B_4*SHRIMP$$
$$+ B_5*MELON + error \quad , \qquad \text{(Model R8)}$$

**Regression 3:**

$$COST = B_0 + B_1*SALAD + B_2*LIQUEURS + B_3*FRUIT$$
$$+ B_4*SHRIMP + B_5*MELON + error \quad . \qquad \text{(Model R9)}$$

---

[25] The Excel function that performs this coding is the =IF function. The entries in row 6 of columns G, H, and I are =IF (D6 = 1,1,0), =IF(D6 = 2,1,0), and =IF (D6 = 3,1,0) respectively, and these entries can be copied for all observations (including the forecasts).

[26] Although most of the regression coefficients in the three models are represented by the same symbol, the actual values of $B_0$ will differ in models R7, R8, and R9, as will those of $B_1$, etc.

## Table 4.16

**Regression Number 3**
Dependent Variable: COST/PERSON

| | Constant | | SALAD | LIQUEURS | FRUIT | SHRIMP | MELON | Y(est) |
|---|---|---|---|---|---|---|---|---|
| Regr. Coef. | 471.6 | | 18.15 | 11.10 | (374.7) | (354.6) | (368.0) | 115 |
| Std. Error | 0.0 | | 2.01 | 2.00 | 0.0 | 0.0 | 0.0 | 135 |
| t value | #DIV/0! | | 9.0 | 5.6 | #DIV/0! | #DIV/0! | #DIV/0! | 122 |

| | | | | | |
|---|---|---|---|---|---|
| # of obs = | 35 | *Deg of F =* | *29* | | |
| R-squared = | 0.8728 | *Resid SD =* | *5.796* | | |

**Regression Number 2**
Dependent Variable: COST/PERSON

| | Constant | | SALAD | LIQUEURS | | SHRIMP | MELON | Y(est) |
|---|---|---|---|---|---|---|---|---|
| Regr. Coef. | 96.94 | | 18.15 | 11.10 | | 20.08 | 6.665 | 115 |
| Std. Error | 2.08 | | 1.98 | 1.97 | | 2.38 | 2.336 | 135 |
| t value | 46.7 | | 9.2 | 5.7 | | 8.4 | 2.9 | 122 |

| | | | | | |
|---|---|---|---|---|---|
| # of obs = | 35 | *Deg of F =* | *30* | | |
| R-squared = | 0.8728 | *Resid SD =* | *5.699* | | |

**Regression Number 1**
Dependent Variable: COST/PERSON

| | Constant | | SALAD | LIQUEURS | FRUIT | SHRIMP | | Y(est) |
|---|---|---|---|---|---|---|---|---|
| Regr. Coef. | 103.6 | | 18.15 | 11.10 | (6.665) | 13.42 | | 115 |
| Std. Error | 2.1 | | 1.98 | 1.97 | 2.336 | 2.51 | | 135 |
| t value | 49.1 | | 9.2 | 5.7 | (2.9) | 5.4 | | 122 |

| | | | | | |
|---|---|---|---|---|---|
| # of obs = | 35 | *Deg of F =* | *30* | | |
| R-squared = | 0.8728 | *Resid SD =* | *5.699* | | |

After each of the regressions was performed, $Y_{est}$ and Residuals were calculated, and the values of $Y_{est}$ were copied to the right of their respective regression outputs. In all three regressions of Table 4.16, the forecasts are identical. Why?

The interpretation of the regression coefficients of a system of dummy variables representing all but one of the possible values of a categorical variable is that the omitted variable represents a "base case" relative to which the effects of the other variables are measured. Thus, in Regression 1 (based on model R7), the base case is Melon; the regression coefficient for Fruit indicates that the estimated cost per person will be 6.665 (cents) less if the appetizer was Fruit instead of Melon, and similarly the estimated cost will be 13.42 more for Shrimp. It follows that the estimated cost of Shrimp will be 13.42 − (6.66) = 20.08 more than for Fruit.

Turning to Regression 2 (based on model R8) in Table 4.16 where Fruit is the base case, we find that the estimated cost of Shrimp is 20.08 more than Fruit, and Melon is 6.665 more; these results are completely consistent with those of Regression 1. Notice that the constants in Regressions 1 and 2 are 103.6 and 96.94, respectively, a difference of 6.66. How do you explain this difference? Can you now explain why both regressions give you the same forecast?

In Regression 3 (based on model R9) all three dummy variables representing appetizers were used. As you can see, the regression coefficients for the dummy variables representing appetizers are all large negative numbers, the constant term is a large positive number, but Shrimp is still 20.1 more costly than Fruit, and Melon is still 6.7 cheaper. Relative to Regression 2, where Fruit represented the base case, the constant is 374.7 higher. Again, the forecasts are identical with those of the preceding regressions.

Notice that in Regression 3 the standard errors of the regression coefficients are reported as 0.0 and the $t$ values indicate an attempt to divide by 0. This should signal that some sort of error has taken place, and indeed one has. Although the computer has come up with a set of regression coefficients that provide forecasts identical with those of Regressions 1 and 2, the regression coefficients are not unique. For instance, if we added 10 to the regression coefficients for each of the appetizer dummy variables and subtracted 10 from the constant term, we would get identical estimates and forecasts. (Try it!) Indeed, if we added *any* constant amount to each of those regression coefficients and subtracted that amount from the constant term, the forecasts and estimates would be the same. In this formulation we have absolutely no idea what the "correct" values of the estimated regression coefficients should be. They are completely unstable, and their standard errors *should* be reported as "infinite."[27]

Regression 3 shows the results of a *misspecified* regression model. The problem is that one of the independent variables in the regression can be expressed as a *linear function* of one or more (in this case two) other independent variables in the regression. For instance,

$$\text{Fruit} = 1 - \text{Shrimp} - \text{Melon}\ :$$

if the appetizer was a shrimp cocktail, then Shrimp=1, Melon=0, and the value of Fruit is necessarily 0, for example.

This is an extreme form of a problem that we shall encounter in less severe form in other regression analyses. It is called **collinearity** or **multicollinearity.** In its extreme form, it occurs when one independent variable is a linear function of one or more other independent variables in the regression. In that case, the regression coefficients are unstable, and the remedy is to drop one of the collinear independent variables from the regression. For that reason, when we create a system of dummy variables representing the various levels of a categorical variable, we always use *one less* dummy variable than the number of categories.

## ▼ Ordinal Independent Variables

Suppose we have as an independent variable in a regression the level of agreement that various respondents have with some statement, classified into five levels: Disagree Strongly, Disagree, Neutral, Agree, and Agree Strongly, with the possible responses coded 1 through 5. Should we use the variable, coded in this way, directly in the regression, or should we transform it? If you use it directly, you are implicitly assuming that the effect on $Y_{est}$ of going from "Strongly Disagree:" to "Disagree" is the same as going from "Disagree" to "Neutral," etc. Can we tell if such an assumption is justified?

---

[27] Many regression programs will simply refuse to give any regression output in situations like this, or will provide output that obviously makes no sense. In our case, the regression utility reports the standard error as 0.0 instead of "infinity."

One way to find out is to create a system of five dummy variables, one for each possible response, and to use four of them as independent variables. Suppose "Disagree Strongly" were the base case, and the estimated regression coefficients for the other responses were 3.5, 6.4, 9.3, and 13.2. That suggests that $Y_{est}$ increases by (roughly) 3.3 units each time you move up one notch on the agreement scale. In that case, it would be reasonable for you to use the original ordinal variable, with values coded as 1 through 5, as an independent variable, thereby saving three degrees of freedom and simplifying the description of how the variables in the model are related. If, on the other hand, the estimated regression coefficients did not move up in roughly equal increments, you would undoubtedly fit the data better by using the four dummy variables, provided you had enough degrees of freedom.

# EXERCISES ON FORECASTING WITH REGRESSION

1. Use data file HOUSES.XLS to forecast the selling price of a 1,654-square-foot 34-year-old house. How sure are you about your forecast?

2. Produce scatter diagrams of Selling Price vs. Area, Selling Price vs. Age, and Area vs. Age. Perform a regression with Selling Price as the dependent and Age as the independent variable. Why is the regression coefficient on Age so small, as compared with its magnitude when Area is also included as an independent variable?

3. Data file ANSCOMBE.XLS contains data on a number of variables. Perform the following regressions:

|     | INDEPENDENT VARIABLE | DEPENDENT VARIABLE |
|-----|----------------------|--------------------|
| a)  | $x_1$                | $y_1$              |
| b)  | $x_1$                | $y_2$              |
| c)  | $x_1$                | $y_3$              |
| d)  | $x_2$                | $y_4$              |

In each case, plot a scatter diagram of the independent against dependent variable. What, if anything, could you do to obtain better regression results in each of the four regressions?

4. Using data file HBSMBA.XLS, develop a regression model that will predict students' first-year grade-point averages. Be prepared to discuss whether you would use such a model to screen students applying for admission.

# HARMON FOODS, INC.

John MacIntyre, general sales manager of the Breakfast Foods Division of Harmon Foods, Inc., was having difficulty in forecasting the sales of Treat. Treat was a ready-to-eat breakfast cereal with an important share of the market. It was the main product in those company plants that manufactured it. MacIntyre was responsible for sales forecasts from which production schedules were prepared. In past months, actual Treat sales had varied from 50% to 200% of his forecast. The greatest difficulty in preparing forecasts arose from the wide variability in historical sales. (See Exhibit 1. Sales were debited on the day of shipment; therefore, Exhibit 1 represents unit shipments as well as sales. Consumer Packs and Dealer Allowances, which are discussed later, are also shown in Exhibit 1.)

## Manufacturing Problems

Accurate production forecasts were essential for the health of the entire business. The plant managers received these forecast schedules and certified their ability to meet them. A plant manager's acceptance of a schedule represented a promise to deliver: crews and machines were assigned, materials ordered, and storage space allocated to meet the schedule.

Schedule changes were expensive. On the one hand, the lead time on raw material orders was several weeks, so that ordering too little not only caused expensive shortages in lost production time but also disappointed customers. Reducing schedules, on the other hand, created a surplus of raw material. Lack of storage space required materials to be left on the trucks, railroad cars, or barges that brought them. Retaining these vehicles resulted in expensive demurrage charges.[28]

Overshadowing the storage problem was the problem of efficient use of the work force. Tight production schedules prevented unnecessary costs. Overtime was avoided because it was expensive and interfered with weekend maintenance. The labor force was highly skilled and difficult to increase in the short run. Layoffs, however, were avoided to preserve the crew's skills. This job security was an important part of the company's labor policy, and it created high employee morale. Thus, the production manager attempted to make production schedules efficient for a constant-size work force while using as little overtime as possible.

Harvard Business School case 9-171-248. This case was prepared by William Whiston.
Copyright © 1970 by the President and Fellows of Harvard College.

[28] Demurrage charges are assessments made by a carrier against a consignee for delays in the unloading (or the initiation of unloading) of a transport vehicle. Usually one free hour is allowed after the normal unloading time for trucks. Railcars and barges have typical allowances of three days and one day, respectively, including unloading time. Charges for delays beyond these allowances range from $20 an hour for a truck and $32 a day for a railcar to $4,000 a day for a barge.

## Advertising Expenditures

Inaccurate sales forecasts also reduced the effectiveness of Treat's advertising expenditures. Most of Treat's advertising dollars were spent on Saturday morning network shows for children. This time was purchased up to a year or more in advance and cost $80,000 per one-minute commercial. The brand managers in the Breakfast Foods Division, however, believed that these network programs delivered the best value for each advertising dollar spent. This opinion was based upon cost per million messages delivered, viewer-recall scores, and measures of audience composition.

Like many other companies, Harmon Foods budgeted advertising expenditures at a fixed amount per unit sold. Each year the monthly budgets for advertising were established, based on forecast sales. Brand managers tended to contract for time on network programs to the limit of their budget allowance. When shipments ran high, however, brand managers tended to increase advertising expenditures in proportion to actual sales. In such circumstances, they would seek contracts for time from other brand managers who were shipping below budget. Failing this, they would seek network time through the agencies, or if such time were unavailable, they would seek spot advertising as close to prime program time as possible. Thus, unplanned advertising expenditures could result in time that gave lower value per advertising dollar spent than did prime time.

## Budgets and Controls

The controller of the Breakfast Foods Division also complained about forecasting errors. Each brand manager prepared a budget based on forecast shipments. This budget promised a contribution to division overhead and profits. Long-term dividend policy and corporate expansion plans were partly based on these forecasts. Regular quarterly increases in earnings over prior years had resulted in a high price-earnings ratio for the company. Because the owners were keenly interested in the market value of the common stock, profit planning played an important part in the management control system.

Discretionary overspending on advertising, noted earlier, amplified the problems of profit planning. These expenditures did not have budgetary approval, and until a new budget base (sales forecast) for the fiscal year was approved at all levels, such overspending was merely borrowing ahead on the current fiscal year. The controller's office charged only the budgeted advertising to sales in each quarter and carried the excess over, because it was unauthorized. This procedure resulted in spurious accounting profits in those quarters where sales exceeded forecast, with counterbalancing profit reductions in subsequent quarters.

The significant effect of deferred advertising expenditures on profits had been demonstrated in the past fiscal year. Treat and several other brands had overspent extensively in the early quarters; as a result, divisional earnings for the fourth quarter were more than $4 million below corporate expectations. The division manager, her sales manager, brand managers, and controller had felt very uncomfortable in the meetings that were held because of this shortage of reported profits. The extra profits recorded in earlier quarters had offset the shortages of other divisions, but in the final quarter, no division was able to offset the Breakfast Foods shortage.

## The Brand Manager

Donald Carswell, the brand manager for Treat, prepared his brand's budget base—a set of monthly, quarterly, and annual forecasts that governed monthly advertising and promotional expenditures. These forecasts, along with forecasts from the division's other brand managers, were submitted to MacIntyre for approval. This approval was necessary because, in a given month, the salesforce could only support the promotions of a limited number of brands. Once approved, the brand managers' forecasts were the basis for MacIntyre's official forecasts.

The production schedule, in turn, was based upon MacIntyre's official forecast. This required mutual confidence and understanding. MacIntyre provided information on Harmon's and also competitors' activities and pricings at the stores. The brand managers furnished knowledge of market trends for their brands and their brands' competitors. The brand managers also kept records of all available market research reports on their brands and similar brands and were aware of any package design and product formulations under development.

As Treat's brand manager, Carswell knew that it was his responsibility to improve the reliability of sales forecasts for Treat. After talking to analysts in the Market Research, Systems Analysis, and Operations Research departments, he concluded that better forecasts were possible. Robert Haas of the Operations Research Department offered to work with him on the project. MacIntyre and the controller enthusiastically supported Carswell's undertaking. Although such projects were outside the normal scope of a brand manager's duties, Carswell recognized this as an opportunity to find a solution to his forecasting problem that would have company-wide application.

## Factors Affecting Sales

Carswell and Haas delved into the factors that influenced sales. A 12-month moving average of the data in Exhibit 1 indicated a long-term rising trend in sales. This trend confirmed the A.C. Nielsen store audit, which reported a small but steady rise in market share for Treat and a steady rise for the commodity group to which Treat belonged.

Besides trend, Carswell felt that seasonal factors might be important. In November and December, sales slowed down as inventory levels among stores and jobbers were drawn down for year-end inventories. Summer sales were often low because of plant shutdowns and sales personnel vacations. There were fewer selling days in February. Salespeople often began the fiscal year with a burst of energy, jockeying for a strong quota position for the rest of the year. Carswell obtained data made available by the National Association of Cereal Manufacturers, showing seasonal effects on shipments of breakfast cereals in the United States. These indexes appear in Exhibit 2.

Nonmedia promotions, which represented about 25% of Treat's advertising budget, strongly influenced sales. The two main types of promotions were consumer packs and dealer allowances. Promotions targeted directly at the consumer were called consumer packs, so named because the consumer was reimbursed in some way for each package of Treat that was purchased. Promotions that sought to increase sales by encouraging the dealer to push the brand were called dealer allowances, so called because allowances were made to dealers to compensate them for expenditures incurred in promoting Treat.

Consumer packs and dealer allowances were each offered two or three times a year during different canvass periods. (A sales canvass period is the time required for a salesperson to make a complete round to all customers in the assigned area. Harmon Foods scheduled ten five-week canvass periods each year. The remaining two weeks, one at mid-summer and one at year-end, were for holidays and vacations.)

## Consumer Packs

Consumer packs were usually a twenty-cent-per-package reduction in the price the consumer paid. The promotion could also be made as a coupon, an enclosed premium, or a mail-in offer. Based on the results of consumer-panel tests of all such promotions, however, Carswell was confident that these forms were roughly equivalent to the twenty-cent price reduction in its return to the brand. Consequently, he decided not to make a distinction among the different kinds of consumer packs. (Exhibit 1 shows the history of consumer pack shipments.)

Consumer packs, supporting advertising material, and special cartons were produced before the assigned canvass period for shipment throughout the five-week period. Any packs not shipped within this period would be allocated among the salespeople for shipment in periods in which no consumer promotion was officially scheduled. From a study of historical data that covered several consumer packs, Haas found that approximately 35% of a consumer-pack offering moved out during the first week, 25% during the second week, 15% during the third week, and approximately 10% during each of the fourth and fifth weeks of the canvass period. Approximately 5% was shipped after the promotional period. Because they saw no reason for this historical pattern to change, Haas and Carswell were confident that they could predict with reasonable accuracy future monthly consumer pack shipments.

Total shipments were favorably affected, of course, during the month in which the consumer packs were shipped. Because the consumer ate Treat at a more or less constant rate over time, Carswell was convinced that part of the increase in total shipments resulted from inventory build-ups by jobbers, stores, and consumers. Thus, he thought that the consumer packs might have a negative influence on total shipments in subsequent months as these excess inventories were depleted in the first, or possibly the second, month after the packs were shipped.

## Dealer Allowances

Sales seemed even more sensitive to allowances offered to dealers for cooperative promotional efforts. Participating dealers received a $4 to $8 per case discount on their purchases during the allowance's canvass period.

The total expenditure for dealer allowances during a given promotional canvass period was budgeted in advance. As with consumer packs, any unspent allowances would be allocated to the salespeople for disbursement after the promotional period. The actual weekly expenditures resulting from these allowances followed approximately the same pattern as the one for the shipment of consumer packs. Consequently, Carswell believed that the monthly expenditures resulting from any given schedule of future dealer allowances could also be predicted with reasonable accuracy.

Dealers promoted Treat by using giant, spectacular end-of-aisle displays, newspaper ads, coupons, fliers, and so forth. Such efforts could affect sales dramatically. For example, an end-of-aisle display located near a cash register could do an average of five weeks' business in a single weekend. As with consumer packs, however, Carswell believed that much of the sales increase was attributable to inventory build-ups, and therefore he expected reactions to these build-ups as late as two months after the initial sales increase.

Actual expenditures made for dealer allowances from 1983 to 1987 appear in Exhibit 1.

## Conclusion

Carswell and Haas felt that they had identified, to the best of their abilities, the important factors affecting sales. They knew that competitive advertising and price moves were important but unpredictable, and they wished to restrict their model to variables that could be measured or predicted in advance.

Haas agreed to formulate the model, construct the data matrix, and write an explanation of how the model's solution could be used to evaluate promotional strategies, as well as to forecast sales and shipments. Carswell and Haas would then plan a presentation to divisional managers.

**Exhibit 1**

| Month | Case Shipments* | Consumer Packs (cases)* | Dealer Allowance | Month | Case Shipments* | Consumer Packs (cases)* | Dealer Allowance |
|---|---|---|---|---|---|---|---|
| Jan-83 | #N/A | 0 | $396,776 | Jan-86 | 655,748 | 544,807 | $664,712 |
| Feb-83 | #N/A | 0 | $152,296 | Feb-86 | 270,483 | 43,704 | $536,824 |
| Mar-83 | #N/A | 0 | $157,640 | Mar-86 | 365,058 | 5,740 | $551,560 |
| Apr-83 | #N/A | 0 | $246,064 | Apr-86 | 313,135 | 9,614 | $150,080 |
| May-83 | #N/A | 15,012 | $335,716 | May-86 | 528,210 | 1,507 | $580,800 |
| Jun-83 | #N/A | 62,337 | $326,312 | Jun-86 | 379,856 | 13,620 | $435,080 |
| Jul-83 | #N/A | 4,022 | $263,284 | Jul-86 | 472,058 | 101,179 | $361,144 |
| Aug-83 | #N/A | 3,130 | $488,676 | Aug-86 | 254,516 | 80,309 | $97,844 |
| Sep-83 | #N/A | 422 | $33,928 | Sep-86 | 551,354 | 335,768 | $30,372 |
| Oct-83 | #N/A | 0 | $224,028 | Oct-86 | 335,826 | 91,710 | $150,324 |
| Nov-83 | #N/A | 0 | $304,004 | Nov-86 | 320,408 | 9,856 | $293,044 |
| Dec-83 | #N/A | 0 | $352,872 | Dec-86 | 276,901 | 107,172 | $162,788 |
| Jan-84 | 425,075 | 75,253 | $457,732 | Jan-87 | 455,136 | 299,781 | $32,532 |
| Feb-84 | 315,305 | 15,036 | $254,396 | Feb-87 | 247,570 | 21,218 | $23,468 |
| Mar-84 | 367,286 | 134,440 | $259,952 | Mar-87 | 622,204 | 157 | $4,503,456 |
| Apr-84 | 429,432 | 119,740 | $267,368 | Apr-87 | 429,331 | 12,961 | $500,904 |
| May-84 | 347,874 | 135,590 | $158,504 | May-87 | 453,156 | 333,529 | $0 |
| Jun-84 | 435,529 | 189,636 | $430,012 | Jun-87 | 320,103 | 178,105 | $0 |
| Jul-84 | 299,403 | 9,308 | $388,516 | Jul-87 | 451,779 | 315,564 | $46,104 |
| Aug-84 | 296,505 | 41,099 | $225,616 | Aug-87 | 249,482 | 80,206 | $92,252 |
| Sep-84 | 426,701 | 9,391 | $1,042,304 | Sep-87 | 744,583 | 5,940 | $4,869,952 |
| Oct-84 | 329,722 | 942 | $974,092 | Oct-87 | 421,186 | 36,819 | $376,556 |
| Nov-84 | 281,783 | 1,818 | $301,892 | Nov-87 | 397,367 | 234,562 | $376,556 |
| Dec-84 | 166,391 | 672 | $76,148 | Dec-87 | 269,096 | 71,881 | $552,536 |
| Jan-85 | 629,404 | 548,704 | $0 | | | | |
| Feb-85 | 263,467 | 52,819 | $315,196 | | | | |
| Mar-85 | 398,320 | 2,793 | $703,624 | | | | |
| Apr-85 | 376,569 | 27,749 | $198,464 | | | | |
| May-85 | 444,404 | 21,887 | $478,880 | | | | |
| Jun-85 | 386,986 | 1,110 | $457,172 | | | | |
| Jul-85 | 414,314 | 436 | $709,480 | | | | |
| Aug-85 | 253,493 | 1,407 | $45,380 | | | | |
| Sep-85 | 484,365 | 376,650 | $28,080 | | | | |
| Oct-85 | 305,989 | 122,906 | $111,520 | | | | |
| Nov-85 | 315,407 | 15,138 | $267,200 | | | | |
| Dec-85 | 182,784 | 5,532 | $354,304 | | | | |

* 1 case contains 24 packs

**Exhibit 2**

### Seasonal Indexes for Breakfast Cereals Shipments

| Month | Index |
|---|---|
| January | 113 |
| February | 98 |
| March | 102 |
| April | 107 |
| May | 119 |
| June | 104 |
| July | 107 |
| August | 81 |
| September | 113 |
| October | 97 |
| November | 95 |
| December | 65 |

# HIGHLAND PARK WOOD COMPANY

In early September 1987, George Simpson, sales manager of the Highland Park Wood Company, received an enquiry from Anne Butler, head buyer for Plainview Homes, a major Dallas-area homebuilder. Plainview was proposing to buy one million board feet of framing lumber at a price to be fixed now, for delivery six months later, in March. Butler explained that Plainview was planning to begin the construction, in early March, of 100 homes in a subdivision northeast of Dallas. Plainview would be willing to purchase all of its framing requirements from Highland Park if Simpson could quote an acceptable, firm price now. Because of recent soaring prices of building materials, Plainview was very cost conscious and desired to fix in advance as large a portion of its construction costs as possible.

Highland Park traditionally passed through to the customer its own cost of purchasing lumber thus eliminating the exposure both sides would face if the price were fixed at the time of the order. Butler, however, appeared to be asking Highland Park to assume this price risk by quoting in September for March delivery. She did indicate, though, that Plainview would be willing to pay more than the 5% margin which Highland Park usually commanded on its direct sales. At the same time, she hinted that Plainview expected a competitive price considering the size of the purchase.

## Costing a Normal Deal

Highland Park was a wood retailer; it bought wood in bulk from a saw mill and carried it in inventory to satisfy customer needs. For a sufficiently large order Highland Park could arrange to have the wood shipped directly to the customer's job site.

The current mill price for the wood Plainview was requesting (Southern Pine #2, 2x4) was $279 per thousand board feet. As a "favored" customer of the mill, Highland Park would receive a 4% wholesaler commission but would have to pay $24 per thousand board feet for delivery from the mill. The delivery charge would be the same whether it were delivered to Highland Park's warehouse or directly to the customer's job site. Thus Highland Park's current delivered costs, before profit, was 0.96 x279 + 24=$291.84 per thousand board feet. For the usual retail order, Highland Park would add a markup of 20%, but for a direct shipment order the markup was only 5%. Had Plainview been asking for immediate delivery the company procedure would suggest a price of $291.84 x 1.05 or $306.43. Plainview could not accept current delivery since it did not have its own storage facilities which explained Plainview's proposal to Highland Park.

Harvard Business School case 9-190-013. This case was prepared by Professor David E. Bell.
Copyright © 1989 by the President and Fellows of Harvard College.

## Buy and Hold

One viable possibility was for Highland Park to buy the wood now and store it until the spring. Apart from the nuisance of taking delivery there was the holding cost to be considered and the additional trucking cost from Highland Park to Plainview's job site in March. The additional trucking cost Simpson estimated as $6 per thousand board feet, but the other costs were less clear. Highland Park usually figured storage costs at an annual rate equal to the prime interest rate plus 6%. This was broken down as Highland Park's cost of short-term capital (prime plus 2%), together with factors to cover taxes (1%), insurance (1%) and depreciation (2%). With the prime currently at 11% this implied a holding cost for six months of 8½% or about $26 per thousand board feet.

Simpson was reluctant to go with this alternative partly because an order of this size threatened to strain Highland Park's storage capabilities but also because he believed Plainview would balk at the price associated with this strategy.

## Wait and Buy

The storage problem could be avoided if Highland Park simply waited until March to order the wood from the mill. However this would entail Highland Park bearing a substantial price risk if prices rose between September and March. A review of past prices confirmed Simpson's fears. (See Exhibit 1, columns 2 and 3.) Had Highland Park undertaken such a strategy in 1975, for example, they would have had to pay a price 35% higher in March (1976) than had prevailed in September (1975). On the other hand, in many years the price was substantially lower in the spring than it had been in the fall, which would have allowed Highland Park a substantial profit.

## Hedging

Simpson had ruled out the possibility of trying to pass along the price risk in this deal to a third party such as a bank or a mill. In particular he had ruled out the possibility of hedging in the futures market. Indeed, if it had been possible to hedge away the risk by forward buying, Plainview could have done this directly themselves.

## Forecasting

There was an active forward market in Hem-Fir, a wood grown almost entirely in the western part of North America and not completely substitutable for Southern Pine. Hem-Fir prices and Southern Pine prices were often quite different and did not always fall and rise together. However, Simpson watched the forward prices for Hem-Fir quite closely in the belief that they offered some insight into likely trends in the market conditions for wood in general. Perhaps significantly the forward price for March delivery of Hem-Fir was now considerably lower than the spot price (see Exhibit 1, columns 4 & 5).

Simpson had asked his assistant to see if there was a useful way to use available information to get a better feel for the likely price of Southern Pine in March. The assistant had compiled the data shown in Exhibit 1 but had not been able to interpret their usefulness.

## The Decision

Simpson was perplexed by the historical pricing details his assistant had collected. He was intrigued by the Plainview proposition and regarded the advance purchase with fixed price guarantee as a marketing experiment and potential source of competitive advantage. At the same time he realized that his company's competitive position had not slipped sufficiently to warrant substantial risk taking.

**Exhibit 1**

### Spot and Forward Prices for Southern Pine and Hem-Fir
### ($ per thousand board feet)

| | SOUTHERN PINE SPOT PRICES | | HEM-FIR | | |
| | | | MARCH | SPOT PRICES | |
| YEAR | SEPT | MARCH | FORWARD | SEPT | MARCH |
|------|------|-------|---------|------|-------|
| 1971 | 135 | 147 | 101 | 108 | 118 |
| 1972 | 153 | 175 | 131 | 147 | 183 |
| 1973 | 201 | 158 | 121 | 163 | 168 |
| 1974 | 112 | 119 | 128 | 126 | 125 |
| 1975 | 127 | 171 | 146 | 140 | 165 |
| 1976 | 187 | 183 | 173 | 180 | 195 |
| 1977 | 264 | 226 | 193 | 218 | 235 |
| 1978 | 225 | 237 | 196 | 246 | 238 |
| 1979 | 303 | 210 | 235 | 293 | 210 |
| 1980 | 197 | 214 | 191 | 194 | 195 |
| 1981 | 170 | 203 | 176 | 178 | 173 |
| 1982 | 191 | 280 | 159 | 163 | 222 |
| 1983 | 222 | 258 | 195 | 189 | 227 |
| 1984 | 202 | 212 | 146 | 177 | 178 |
| 1985 | 212 | 244 | 145 | 188 | 220 |
| 1986 | 215 | 242 | 172 | 232 | 238 |
| 1987 | 277 | | 182 | 240 | |

### Explanation:

***Spot.*** The price of Southern Pine at the beginning of September 1971 was $135 per thousand board feet. The price of Southern Pine at the beginning of the *following* March was $147. Similarly, the price of Hem-Fir at the beginning of September 1971 was $108 per thousand board feet. The *following* March, the price had climbed to $118.

***Forward.*** In early September 1971 the current price of Hem-Fir if delivered in March 1972, was $101 per thousand board feet. (For the purpose of this case, it suffices to think of these figures as market forecasts, as of September of the given year, for Hem-Fir prices the *following* March.)

# CAUSAL INFERENCE

## INTRODUCTION

In Chapter 4, *Forecasting with Regression Analysis*, we saw how you could use regression analysis to forecast a future value of a dependent variable. In this chapter we take up a second use of regression: causal inference. We use regression to infer by how much a deliberate intervention that changes the value of some independent variable will *cause* the value of the dependent variable to change. For example, we may be interested in how much our company's stock price will change if we increase our dividend by $1, or how much gross domestic product changes if the Fed lowers interest rates by 1%, or how sales will change after an increase of $1 million in advertising expenditures. Sometimes you can infer these causal effects by examining past data. When such data are "observational" (not obtained from carefully controlled experiments), you can use the regression model to estimate those effects.

Many textbooks in statistics assert that you cannot infer causation from observational data; rather, you can only infer statistical association. They state that you might observe in a representative sample of data that whenever $x$ increases by one unit, $y$ increases by three units, on average, but from that you cannot conclude that the expected value of $y$ will necessarily increase by three units (or at all) if you deliberately cause $x$ to increase by one unit.

Contrast this with what managers, scientists, and economists do. A manager of a fast-food chain might observe that restaurants located near a McDonald's restaurant do better than those that are not near a McDonald's, and as a result will seek new restaurant sites near McDonald's. A doctor may observe that patients who smoke incur heart and lung disease at a higher rate than nonsmokers, and therefore advise her patients not to smoke. An economist may observe that high inflation is associated with low unemployment and vice versa, and recommend that to control inflation the government should take steps to increase unemployment. These are all violations of the textbook rule.

In this chapter, we show how you can sometimes infer from observational data how changing the value of one variable causes the value of some other variable to change. You will see that although you cannot "prove" causation, you may be able to make reasonable causal inferences. But you can easily make incorrect inferences unless you are very careful.

Harvard Business School note 894-032. This note was prepared by Professor Arthur Schleifer, Jr.
Copyright © 1994 by the President and Fellows of Harvard College.

# WHAT IS CAUSATION?

An assertion that reducing the price of a product from $18 per unit to $17 *causes* demand to increase from 22,000 units per month to 23,000 makes sense only in terms of an ideal experiment—one that can never be performed in practice. The experiment involves two scenarios. In the first, price is set at $18. The second scenario is identical to the first in all respects except that the price is set at $17. Under both scenarios, the monthly demand is observed. If demand was 22,000 units per month when price was $18, and 23,000 when price was $17, we can conclude that the price change *caused* the change in demand.

"Identical in all respects . . ." means just that. The two scenarios cannot take place in different periods of time, or in different geographical regions. Although it is common practice to assert that an increase in demand that followed a reduction in price was "caused" by the price reduction, such an assertion involves measurement of demand in two different periods, between which other factors that affect demand may have changed.

Given that the "ideal" experiment can never be performed in practice, we can never measure exactly how much a change in the value of one variable causes the value of another variable to change. Our challenge is to find methods that come as close as possible to mimicking the ideal experiment. But before discussing such methods, let's explore what we would learn if we could actually carry out this two-scenario experiment.

The price reduction—the variable whose value we deliberately change—is called a **treatment** or an **intervention**. What is the effect of that treatment? Although we have focused on just one effect that was of particular interest to us—the change in demand—it should be clear that the price change causes not just this one effect, but many effects. An increase in demand of 1,000 units next month means that some customers who would not have purchased at the old price decided to purchase as a result of the intervention. This, in turn, may mean that some of them will not purchase some other product, and that some will reduce their savings or increase their debt. Perhaps a competitor will respond to our price reduction by reducing his price as well (something he would not have done had we not lowered our price), and this too might have an impact on the demand for our product.

Some of those effects may have little to do with our "bottom line," but others may. If lowering the price of one item in our product line diverts demand away from other items, then the total effect of the intervention is the increase in demand for the item whose price was reduced, less the decrease in demand for substitute products. This is more appropriately measured in dollars than in units. A single intervention usually can change the values of many variables, but one of them—the net change in dollar sales across all items in our product line—is the one we select to be the **dependent variable**, the one that most appropriately measures the total effect of the intervention.

# WHAT IS AN EXPERIMENT?

The nearest we can come in the real world to measuring the true effect of a treatment is to conduct an experiment by finding "matched pairs"—pairs of individuals (or experimental units) that are as alike as possible in all respects—and to apply the treatment to one member of the pair and not to the other. If the pairs were truly matched in all respects, we could achieve with matched pairs what the "ideal experiment" does with a single individual or experimental unit:

measure the effect by measuring the difference in their responses. Unfortunately, from a practical point of view, it is not possible to find individuals who are exactly alike in all respects. (Even identical twins have almost certainly been exposed to different environmental influences.) Thus "matched pairs" may be alike in many respects, but they may differ with respect to other, unmeasured variables that have an effect on the dependent variable. If these unmeasured variables happen to be correlated with the treatment, the observed treatment effect will include a **proxy effect** for these other variables.

Even the choice of which experimental unit gets the treatment and which does not may make it difficult to sort out effects. For example, the average effect on longevity of giving up smoking (the "treatment") may be different for people who voluntarily give it up than for people who are forced to give it up. In the extreme, we could imagine a situation in which those who voluntarily give up smoking are the only ones whose longevity is increased. If this were true, we would observe that those who gave up smoking lived longer than those who did not, but we would also discover that applying coercion or providing incentives to nonvolunteers to give up smoking would provide no benefits to them.

Unwanted proxy effects of unmeasured variables can be eliminated by using a random device to choose which experimental unit in a matched pair receives the treatment. Random assignment of treatments assures that, on average, whatever unmeasured variables affect the dependent variable will not be correlated with the treatment. Thus, the treatment will not capture unwanted proxy effects.

There are situations where this random assignment can be carried out relatively easily. Returning to our price-reduction problem, suppose the context is that of a direct-mail company. The company could prepare two sets of catalogs, both identical except for the item whose price reduction was under consideration. One set of catalogs would show the standard price; the other set, the reduced price. Matched pairs of customers could be selected based on the recency, frequency, and monetary value of their previous purchases, and for each pair the catalog with the reduced price could be assigned at random. In drug testing, it is routine to assign the drug to one member of a matched pair, and a placebo to the other, with the determination of who gets what decided by a randomizing device (e.g., the flip of a coin).

There are other situations where random assignment is virtually impossible, either because it is too hard to implement or because it is socially unacceptable. In the smoking experiment, it would be impossible to justify and enforce a policy in which some people, chosen at random, were instructed to keep smoking, while others were told to stop smoking. In dealing with the economy, we cannot segment the population into two groups, and take measures to increase unemployment among only one group, then observe the difference in the rate of inflation in the two segments. Even in the pricing example, the mail-order company's management might find it unacceptable to have two catalogs with different prices in circulation. We are often reduced to relying on observational data.

# OBSERVATIONAL DATA

When we seek to estimate from observational data the effect of a "treatment"— an independent variable whose value we will be able to manipulate in the future—on a dependent variable, the estimation problem is made more difficult by the presence of other independent variables that may also affect the dependent variable, and may be correlated with the treatment variable.

An independent variable may be correlated with the treatment for one of four reasons:

1.   There may be no causal relationship between the two variables, but they might be correlated by chance alone.

2.   The independent variable may **affect** the treatment.

3.   It may be **affected by** the treatment.

4.   It and the treatment may both be affected by some other variable: they may be correlated due to a "common cause."

## An Example

We may, for example, be interested in learning by how much changes in the posted speed limit on highways (the treatment) affect motor-vehicle death rates—deaths per thousand drivers per year (the dependent variable). The reason for our interest is that if we discover that reducing the speed limit reduces death rates, we might want to propose legislation to lower the speed limit.

Suppose we have a cross section of the fifty states in the United States, with data on each state's maximum speed limit and motor-vehicle death rate. Even if lowering the speed limit really reduced the death rate, a scatter diagram of speed limit vs. death rate might show that, in the data, death rate declines as speed limit increases. How could this be? It might be that states with very high death rates are states where bad weather makes driving conditions hazardous, where drivers drive long distances, where driving under the influence of alcohol is prevalent, etc. These states may have lowered the speed limit to reduce the carnage, but still have higher death rates than states in which driving is safer, but the speed limit remains high. If this story is correct, then low speed limits may reduce the death rate but also proxy for variables that increase the death rate.

If those other variables—weather conditions, miles driven per capita per year, alcohol consumption, etc.—are included, along with speed limit, as independent variables in a regression model, then the regression coefficient on speed limit will show how death rate varies with speed limit when the other variables in the model are held constant. Speed limit will no longer proxy for these other variables. If lower speed limits reduce the death rate, then the regression coefficient on speed limit will be negative. Weather conditions, miles driven, and alcohol consumption are examples of other independent variables that *affect* death rate and that are *correlated* with speed limit. The correlation occurs because these variables have *caused* the speed limit to be lowered in states where they are major contributors to highway deaths. These variables *should* be included in the model to eliminate their unwanted proxy effects on the treatment variable.

Suppose we discover that states whose citizens have pronounced concerns for public safety tend to have both low speed limits and rigorous automobile-inspection standards. This is a case where the treatment and another variable (automobile inspection) that may affect death rates are correlated because they are both affected by another variable that is a **common cause**—concern for public safety. Clearly, a measure of the rigor of inspection standards should be included as an independent variable; otherwise, speed limit will capture the unwanted proxy effect of inspection on death rate.[1]

---

[1] If inspection and speed are perfectly correlated, it will be impossible to sort out to what degree each contributes to lowering the death rate. This is an example of **collinearity**, a problem that occurs frequently in regression. Collinearity is not a defect in the methodology; it is a defect in the data. The only way you can sort out the effects in this extreme case is to change the relationship between speed limit and inspection in the data.

Now suppose that reduction in the posted speed limit causes drivers to drive slower, on average, and it is the actual reduction in speed driven, not the posted speed limit, that causes the death rate to decrease. Should we include average speed driven as an independent variable in our model? Clearly not: if we did, the regression coefficient on posted speed limit would show its relationship to death rate when average speed driven remained constant, and since actual speed driven, not posted speed limit, causes fatal accidents, the coefficient would indicate that the effect of posted speed limit on death rate was zero, and thus make it appear that changing posted speed has no effect on death rate. To assure that the regression coefficient correctly captures the causal relationship, we want posted speed limit to *include* the "good" proxy effect of driving speed, and thus we want to *exclude* driving speed from the regression model. Driving speed is an example of a variable that affects the dependent variable but is *affected by* the treatment variable. Such a variable should be excluded from the model, so that the treatment variable will capture its proxy effects.

Finally, consider the case where some other variable, say the average age of cars in the various states, affects death rates, but has no causal relationship to posted speed limits. Nonetheless, average age may be correlated with speed limits in the sample data: even variables that have nothing to do with one another are seldom perfectly uncorrelated in observational data. In this case, failure to include average age of cars as an independent variable in the model will cause speed limit to carry an unwanted proxy effect for age of cars. We should, therefore, *include* age of cars as an independent variable.

# WHICH INDEPENDENT VARIABLES SHOULD BE INCLUDED?

Based on this example, we can state the following rules. When you want to estimate the effect that a treatment or intervention will have on a dependent variable, you should:

- include as an independent variable any variable that you believe might affect the dependent variable and that is correlated with the treatment variable because (a) it affects the treatment variable, or (b) both the dependent variable and the treatment variable are affected by a common cause, or (c) the correlation occurred purely by chance.
- exclude from the model any variable that you believe might affect the dependent variable and that is correlated with the treatment variable because it is affected by the treatment variable.

If a variable affects the dependent variable but is uncorrelated with the treatment variable, whether you include it or not makes no difference in the regression coefficient for the treatment variable: there are no proxy effects from an uncorrelated variable. As a matter of practice, you should include any variable that affects the treatment variable; at the very least, it will improve the fit of the model. In a sample of observational data only rarely are two variables completely uncorrelated.

The consequences of these rules may seem counterintuitive. A variable that affects the dependent variable and is correlated with the treatment variable must be included in the model; the higher the correlation, the more important it is to include it. Including such a variable will not greatly improve the fit (increase $R^2$, decrease RSD). Nevertheless, omitting a variable like this distorts the apparent effect of the treatment variable by causing it to pick up the unwanted proxy effects of the omitted variable.

On the other hand, omitting an independent variable that affects the dependent variable and is affected by the treatment variable assures that the treatment variable captures its "good" proxy effects. Nevertheless, omitting such a variable invariably results in a poorer fit (lower $R^2$, higher RSD).

In both cases, what is good for proper causal inference is bad for forecasting. This seemingly counterintuitive result is resolved by recognizing that causal inference involves correctly estimating a particular regression coefficient, while forecasting involves providing a good fit to past data. What is good practice for dealing with one of these problems is not necessarily good practice for dealing with the other.

# How to Identify the Relevant Independent Variables

Given that you should include any independent variable that might affect the dependent variable and that is correlated with the treatment variable, but is not affected by it, how do you decide what variables to include? The answer depends on your understanding of what causes what, and on your ingenuity in finding ways of measuring crucial variables. Sometimes you have to settle for a variable that is correlated with such a crucial variable. In our speed-limit example, you may have trouble obtaining data on drunk-driving convictions in a state, but probably can easily get statistics on alcohol consumption. For many reasons this may be an imperfect measure of driving under the influence, but it may be good enough for our purposes. Think about how you would measure weather conditions that are dangerous for drivers, or amount of driving per person.

A useful tool for depicting causal relationships is the **influence diagram**. Figure 5.1 shows such a diagram schematically. A treatment variable and a dependent variable are shown. Other variables are classified by type. Type A variables affect the dependent variable directly as well as indirectly through their effect on the treatment variable. Type B variables affect the dependent variable and are correlated with the treatment variable by virtue of a common cause. Type C variables affect the dependent variable and are correlated with the treatment variable by chance. Type D variables affect the dependent variable but are uncorrelated with the treatment variable. All of these variables should be included as independent variables in the regression model.

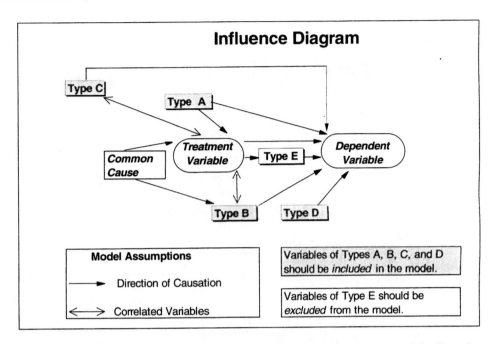

**Figure 5.1**

Type E variables, on the other hand, affect the dependent variable directly, but are affected in turn by the treatment variable. They should not be included in the model.

It is not always clear which way the causation goes. Advertising expenditures by your competitor may be correlated with your advertising. The correlation may be due to a common cause (seasonality, business conditions), in which case your competitor's advertising should be included as an independent variable. On the other hand, your competitor may simply be reacting to your advertising, raising expenditures when you raise yours, and vice versa, in which case it should be excluded. About all you can do under such circumstances is perform the regression with and without the competitive-advertising variable, and weight the resulting regression coefficients on the treatment variable by the probability you assign to the two competing causal models.

# EXERCISE ON CAUSAL INFERENCE

In 1976 the Federal Trade Commission (FTC) launched an investigation to provide insight into the question of whether test preparation centers such as Stanley H. Kaplan have a reasonable basis for claiming they help students increase their Scholastic Aptitude Test (SAT) scores.

The data base KAPLAN.XLS contains observations on 246 high school students who took the test twice. Some of these students were coached by Kaplan or some other test preparation center between the first and second administration of the test. The variables consist of SAT scores, demographics, high-school-performance indicators, and whether or not coaching occurred.

What do you conclude about the effectiveness of coaching?

# NOPANE ADVERTISING STRATEGY

Nopane was a mature proprietary drug product which had been marketed for a decade. Nopane's marketing program had undergone little change for some time when a new product manager, Alison Silk, assumed responsibility for the brand.

Silk undertook a careful review of the brand's history and available marketing research information. There were 12 competing brands, four of which, accounting for 60% of the market, were nationally distributed and supported by media advertising. Nopane was an important but not dominant brand among the four, with a 15% share of market. No consumer promotion (dealing, couponing, etc.) was used to any appreciable extent and price cutting was negligible, but all four major brands were priced above the level of the remaining brands in the category, and all four advertised heavily.

After working on Nopane for several months, Silk became convinced that sales could be increased by repositioning the brand. The brand's advertising agency prepared and tested some new approaches in focus group interviews. The results were quite favorable.

Encouraged, Silk authorized the agency to produce television commercials, to be aired on local TV stations, representing two different advertising strategies, one emphasizing what was labeled an "*emotional*" appeal, the other a "*rational*" approach. Silk planned a market test to reveal which one to use in a national roll-out at a later stage. Silk was also uncertain about what level of advertising was needed to support the strategy change. After consulting with the Marketing Research Manager, Silk proposed that an advertising experiment be conducted to address the following issues:

1. Do the "emotional" and "rational" copy alternatives differ in their effectiveness?

2. What level of advertising should be used for Nopane for the coming fiscal year?

## Experimental Design

Two elements of the advertising campaign were to be systematically varied: copy and media spending. Two copy treatments ("emotional" and "rational") and three levels of advertising intensity were to be tested. Expressed in six-month expenditures per 100 "prospects" (potential customers) in a geographical area, the levels to be tested were $2.50, $4.75, and $8.00. The company had divided the U.S. into two segments; Segment A consisted of states lying along the east and west coasts of the United States while the rest of the country comprised Segment B. The two segments contained about equal numbers of total prospects. Twelve sales territories (out of a total of 75) were selected at random from the region designated as Segment A and another twelve were selected from Segment B. The complete experimental design, therefore, provided 24 observations (2 segments * 2 copy executions * 3 levels of media expenditure * 2 test territories).

Harvard Business School case 9-893-005. This case was prepared by Professor David E. Bell.

Sales measurements were obtained based on point-of-sale information in each of the territories. The experiment was run for six months, a period known from prior investigations to be sufficient for the long-term response to advertising to become clear. Arrangements were made to monitor competitive advertising activity in each of the 24 test territories.

## Experiment Results

Exhibit 1 shows the results of the experiment. The 24 rows in the table each reflect one test sales territory. Each row records the segment, copy type, Nopane advertising expenditure, unit sales of Nopane, and competitor advertising expenditure in a territory. The last two columns represent segment and copy as dummy variables (1 = A, 0 = B for segment, 1 = Emotional, 0=Rational for copy type) for the purpose of running regressions.

Silk first regressed Nopane sales against the other variables in the table. (See Regression 1, below.) She was particularly interested, of course, in seeing how sales responded to Nopane advertising expenditure ("Ad Dollars") and to the two ad types ("Dum Copy").

**Regression Number 1**
Dependent Variable: SALES

|  | Ad Dollars | Constant | Competition | Dum Segm | Dum Copy |
|---|---|---|---|---|---|
| Regr. Coef. | 1.477 | 32.59 | (0.5652) | 0.3514 | 2.134 |
| Std. Error | 0.338 | 2.53 | 0.1622 | 1.4005 | 2.027 |
| t value | 4.4 | 12.9 | (3.5) | 0.3 | 1.1 |

| | | | | |
|---|---|---|---|---|
| # of obs = | **24** | Deg of F = | **19** | |
| R-squared = | **0.5889** | Resid SD = | **3.411** | |

## Meeting with the Division Vice-President

On February 7, 1992, Alison presented her conclusions to the Division Vice-President, Stanley Skamarycz, whose approval would be needed for a change in advertising strategy. Alison showed him the experimental data and her regression. She was surprised by his response. "These results are worthless!" he said. "It's clear that our competitors have run interference on your experiment. As you can see, they systematically varied their own advertising strategy across our different test territories."

"It could be," remarked Alison, "that their response mirrors the response they will follow if we go national."

"I doubt it," responded Stanley. "I'd be prepared to bet that no matter which copy we choose, or what media expenditure we pick, they'll spend at a rate of about $19 per 100 prospects per sales territory per six-month period. I say that because that is what they have always done in the past."

# Further Analysis

Back in her office, Silk ran a new regression (Regression 2) that seemed to confirm Skamarycz's theory that the amount of competitor advertising in a sales territory had depended on whether the "emotional" or "rational" advertising strategy had been used by Nopane.

She wrote two hypotheses on a piece of paper:

**Regression Number 2**
Dependent Variable: COMPETITION

|  | Ad Dollars |  | Constant | Dum Segm | Dum Copy |
|---|---|---|---|---|---|
| Regr. Coef. | 0.8515 |  | 9.713 | 0.9167 | 9.083 |
| Std. Error | 0.4251 |  | 2.726 | 1.9196 | 1.920 |
| t value | 2.0 |  | 3.6 | 0.5 | 4.7 |

|  |  |  |  |  |
|---|---|---|---|---|
| # of obs = | **24** | Deg of F = | **20** | |
| R-squared = | **0.5711** | Resid SD = | **4.702** | |

***Silk's Hypothesis*** — Nopane's competitors will react to our national strategy (whatever it might be) in the same way as they did in the test.

***Skamarycz's Hypothesis*** — Whatever our national strategy, we can expect our competitors to spend an average of $19 per 100 prospects per sales territory per six-month period.

Concerned that these two hypotheses might have profoundly different implications for a national advertising strategy for Nopane, she decided to re-run Regression 1 without the "Competitor" variable (see Regression 3).

**Regression Number 3**
Dependent Variable: SALES

|  | Ad Dollars | Constant |  | Dum Segm | Dum Copy |
|---|---|---|---|---|---|
| Regr. Coef. | 0.9959 | 27.10 |  | (0.1667) | (3.000) |
| Std. Error | 0.3848 | 2.47 |  | 1.7376 | 1.738 |
| t value | 2.6 | 11.0 |  | (0.1) | (1.7) |

|  |  |  |  |  |
|---|---|---|---|---|
| # of obs = | **24** | Deg of F = | **20** | |
| R-squared = | **0.3263** | Resid SD = | **4.256** | |

# Exhibit 1

## Results of Experiment

| SEGMENT | COPY | ADVERTISING DOLLARS (per 100 Prospects)<br>AD DOLLARS | UNIT SALES NOPANE (per 100 Prospects)<br>SALES | COMPETITOR ADVERTISING $ (per 100 Prospects)<br>COMPETITION | DUMMY VARIABLES SEGMENT 1 = A 0 = B<br>DUM SEGM | FOR COPY 1 = Emotional 0 = Rational<br>DUM COPY |
|---|---|---|---|---|---|---|
| A | Emotional | 2.50 | 26 | 16 | 1 | 1 |
| A | Emotional | 2.50 | 26 | 20 | 1 | 1 |
| A | Emotional | 4.75 | 31 | 23 | 1 | 1 |
| A | Emotional | 4.75 | 32 | 24 | 1 | 1 |
| A | Emotional | 8.00 | 24 | 25 | 1 | 1 |
| A | Emotional | 8.00 | 31 | 33 | 1 | 1 |
| A | Rational | 2.50 | 25 | 20 | 1 | 0 |
| A | Rational | 2.50 | 26 | 14 | 1 | 0 |
| A | Rational | 4.75 | 32 | 19 | 1 | 0 |
| A | Rational | 4.75 | 35 | 12 | 1 | 0 |
| A | Rational | 8.00 | 40 | 13 | 1 | 0 |
| A | Rational | 8.00 | 38 | 15 | 1 | 0 |
| B | Emotional | 2.50 | 33 | 16 | 0 | 1 |
| B | Emotional | 2.50 | 30 | 15 | 0 | 1 |
| B | Emotional | 4.75 | 35 | 24 | 0 | 1 |
| B | Emotional | 4.75 | 26 | 25 | 0 | 1 |
| B | Emotional | 8.00 | 30 | 28 | 0 | 1 |
| B | Emotional | 8.00 | 25 | 34 | 0 | 1 |
| B | Rational | 2.50 | 26 | 14 | 0 | 0 |
| B | Rational | 2.50 | 25 | 18 | 0 | 0 |
| B | Rational | 4.75 | 30 | 16 | 0 | 0 |
| B | Rational | 4.75 | 33 | 10 | 0 | 0 |
| B | Rational | 8.00 | 38 | 11 | 0 | 0 |
| B | Rational | 8.00 | 37 | 12 | 0 | 0 |

# Explanation of Numerical Variables

Ad Dollars = Number of dollars per 100 prospects spent on Nopane advertising

Sales = Unit sales of Nopane per 100 prospects

Competition = Number of dollars per 100 prospects spent by competitors advertising their own products

Dum Segm = 1 if sales territory is in Segment A
= 0 if sales territory is in Segment B

Dum Copy = 1 if "emotional" copy used
= 0 if "rational" copy used

Note: All sales figures and advertising expenditures are per 100 prospects per six-month period.

# LINCOLN COMMUNITY HOSPITAL

The five-person Executive Committee of the Board of Trustees of the Lincoln Community Hospital, a 180-bed not-for-profit hospital in Sparta, New York (population: 135,000), met Saturday, January 19, 1985, to develop an understanding of the factors driving hospital costs. Lincoln had been incurring an operating deficit (the difference between the hospital's revenues for services rendered and its operating costs) for each of the last six years, its financial position was precarious, and the Executive Committee was under increasing pressure to bring in a for-profit management team. An understanding of hospital costs would be a relevant input to a decision on whether to change management.

Lincoln's case was typical of the predicament facing many not-for-profit community hospitals in the mid-1980s. Faced with rising costs (in part because of the increasing complexity of modern medical care) and lower revenues (primarily because of cost containment by third-party reimbursements of hospital bills, e.g., the government, Blue Cross/Blue Shield, and other medical insurers), many of these hospitals were experiencing persistent and chronic operating deficits. Most not-for-profit community hospitals did not have many beds and could not take advantage of the supposed scale economies in running a hospital. Being independent, these hospitals were also denied the benefits of any scale economies that might result from the management of a large chain of hospitals. Furthermore, they were often the only hospital in the community and could not control the complexity of the mix of cases they took in. Finally, these hospitals had to contend with criticisms alleging that they were not run as efficiently as for-profit hospitals.

The debate at the Executive Committee meeting was heated and inconclusive. Finally, at 9:30 p.m., Dr. Otto Planck, the Committee's chairperson and a former director of the hospital, said: "Let's call it a day. It's clear we have conflicting notions as to what drives hospital costs. Why don't we look at some data to examine the merits of these notions? Since we are all in agreement that Lincoln should not become affiliated with a hospital chain, I will examine the data available on operating costs for other independent hospitals and report back to you next Saturday."

For his analysis, Dr. Planck looked at data for the year 1983 on costs and related variables for 494 independent for-profit and not-for-profit hospitals in the United States. Dr. Planck's analysis is documented in the five regressions in Exhibit 1; the variables used in these regressions are described in Exhibit 2.

Harvard Business School case 9-191-149. This case was prepared by Professor Anirudh Dhebar. It was adapted from the case *Bellevue Hospital* by Professor Richard F. Meyer, which in turn was based on Regina E. Herzlinger and Williams S. Krasker, *Who Profits from Nonprofits?* Harvard Business Review 65, #1 (January - February, 1987), pp. 93-106. The data have been disguised for instructional purposes.

## Exhibit 1

### Regression Outputs

---

**Regression Number 1**
Dependent Variable: Cost

| | Constant | Beds | Patient-Days |
|---|---|---|---|
| Regr. Coef. | (4,722,847) | 119,655 | 114.7 |
| Std. Error | 351,921 | 4,972 | 21.9 |
| t value | (13.4) | 24.1 | 5.2 |

| | | | |
|---|---|---|---|
| # of obs = | **494** | Deg of F = | **491** |
| R-squared = | **0.9153** | Resid SD = | **5,036** |

---

**Regression Number 2**
Dependent Variable: Occupancy

| | For-Pft | Constant |
|---|---|---|
| Regr. Coef. | 30.39 | 189.7 |
| Std. Error | 6.51 | 5.7 |
| t value | 4.7 | 33.1 |

| | | | |
|---|---|---|---|
| # of obs = | **494** | Deg of F = | **492** |
| R-squared = | **0.0424** | Resid SD = | **60.40** |

---

**Regression Number 3**
Dependent Variable: Cost/bed

| | Beds | For-Pft | Constant | Occupancy |
|---|---|---|---|---|
| Regr. Coef. | 182.6 | (15,188) | 30,889 | 225.4 |
| Std. Error | 9.1 | 2,552 | 4,132 | 17.3 |
| t value | 20.1 | (6.0) | 7.5 | 13.0 |

| | | | |
|---|---|---|---|
| # of obs = | **494** | Deg of F = | **490** |
| R-squared = | **0.5383** | Resid SD = | **23,150** |

---

**Regression Number 4**
Dependent Variable: Cost/bed

| | Beds | Casemix | For-Pft | Constant |
|---|---|---|---|---|
| Regr. Coef. | (25.39) | 120,947 | 11,600 | (43,379) |
| Std. Error | 20.73 | 10,845 | 3,145 | 10,829 |
| t value | (1.2) | 11.2 | 3.7 | (4.0) |

| | | | |
|---|---|---|---|
| # of obs = | **494** | Deg of F = | **490** |
| R-squared = | **0.5040** | Resid SD = | **23,990** |

---

**Regression Number 5**
Dependent Variable: Cost/bed

| | Beds | Casemix | For-Pft | Constant | Occupancy |
|---|---|---|---|---|---|
| Regr. Coef. | (17.38) | 117,442 | 4,308 | (82,031) | 220.3 |
| Std. Error | 17.26 | 9,031 | 2,664 | 9,387 | 14.9 |
| t value | (1.0) | 13.0 | 1.6 | (8.7) | 14.8 |

| | | | |
|---|---|---|---|
| # of obs = | **494** | Deg of F = | **489** |
| R-squared = | **0.6570** | Resid SD = | **19,970** |

---

## Exhibit 2

### Variables in Dr. Planck's Data Base

Year of study: 1983
Number of hospitals: 494

| VARIABLE NAME | DESCRIPTION | MINIMUM | AVERAGE | MAXIMUM |
|---|---|---|---|---|
| *NATURAL VARIABLES* | | | | |
| Cost | Total Operating Cost | $755,773 | $14,885,419 | $88,524,179 |
| Beds | Number of beds | 16 | 136 | 562 |
| Patient-days | Number of Patient-days | 1,647 | 28,958 | 140,846 |
| Casemix | Average complexity of cases in hospital | 0.640 | 1.074 | 2.097 |
| For-Profit | 1 if for-profit hospital; 0 if not-for-profit | 0.000 | 0.775 | 1.000 |
| *TRANSFORMATIONS* | | | | |
| Cost/Bed | Operating Cost/ Number of beds | $18,276 | $92,031 | $195,735 |
| Occupancy | Occupancy rate (Patient-days/Beds) | 33.1 | 213.3 | 364.1 |

# MULTIPLICATIVE REGRESSION MODELS

## INTRODUCTION

The standard regression model relates a dependent variable $y$ to an independent variable $x$ using the relationship:

$$y = b_0 + b_1 * x + \text{residual} \quad,$$

so that the estimated value of $y$ is given by:

$$y_{est} = b_0 + b_1 * x \quad.$$

For given values of $b_0$ and $b_1$, this implies that the relationship between $x$ and $y_{est}$ is *linear*. Furthermore, we have assumed that if the regression is correctly specified, the residuals will be indistinguishable. Thus, the frequency distribution of the residuals tells us all we can learn about what the value of a residual on a new observation will be; knowing the value of $x$ (or any other variable not included in the model) on such an observation will not enable us to improve on our prediction of the residual.[1] In particular, the mean and standard deviation of the residuals should not depend on the value of $x$ or of any other variables.

This is often a satisfactory form of model to use when $y$ and $x$ are difference-scale variables, or when $x$ is a dummy variable. It may be good enough even when $x$ and/or $y$ are ratio-scale variables that do not vary over a very large range. For example, we were able to derive a reasonable relationship between weight and height using a linear model.

## AN EXAMPLE

Business and economic data often involve ratio-scale variables that cover a substantial range of values. If this is true the simple linear model may be substantially incorrect for a number of reasons. To see why, let's look at Figure 6.1, which is a scatter diagram relating the yield per acre for an agricultural product (avocados) to its price. The data pertain to California, where most avocados in the United States are grown, and cover the twenty-five years from 1950 through 1974.

Harvard Business School note 9-893-013. This note was prepared by Professor Arthur Schleifer, Jr.

[1] Remember that we use the distribution of residuals to make probabilistic forecasts—see Figure 4.3 in Chapter 4, *Forecasting with Regression Analysis*.

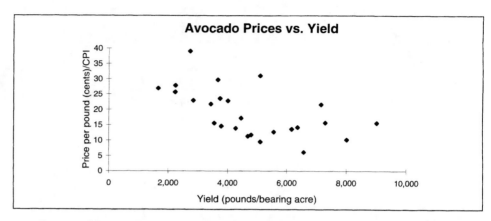

*Figure 6.1*

Crop yield varies considerably from one year to the next largely because of weather and crop diseases. In addition, yields are affected by soil treatment (fertilizers), and the age of the trees. In years of low yield, prices tend to be bid up by people who are willing to pay a premium to obtain avocados that are in short supply. By contrast, in years of high yield, a market surplus tends to drive the price down. Of course, many other factors affect the price of avocados as well. A growing population, the number of acres planted with avocado trees, greater affluence (avocados are a luxury food item), inflation,[2] changes in consumer taste and eating habits, attempts to influence consumers by advertising and promotion, changes in distribution, and competition from foreign growers and from alternate luxury fruits all affect price. Nonetheless, one's general impression from Figure 6.1 is that as yield increases, price tends to decrease, albeit with many exceptions.

A regression with price as the dependent variable and yield as the independent variable results in an estimated constant term $b_0 = 30.59$, and an estimated regression coefficient $b_1 = -0.00241$; the residual standard deviation is 6.65. Figure 6.2 is the same scatter diagram as Figure 6.1 with the estimated regression line superimposed.

The regression line is downward sloping, conforming to our belief that high yields drive prices lower, and the fit is fairly good ($R^2 = 0.33$). We shall return later in this chapter to a more sophisticated analysis of this problem, but for now let's just look at the implications of what we have.

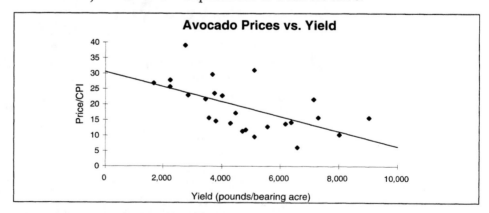

*Figure 6.2*

---

[2] Inflation effects can be taken into account by expressing price in constant cents per pound. This has been done in Figure 6.1 by dividing each year's current price by the value of the consumer price index in that year.

# PROBLEMS WITH THE LINEAR MODEL

We would feel quite comfortable forecasting the price in a year when the yield per acre was 7,500 pounds. By formula, estimated price = 30.59 − 0.00241 *7,500 = 12.52 cents per pound. But what if we want to extrapolate beyond the range of the data? Suppose we anticipate a banner year for crop yield: 13,000 pounds. Our formula then predicts that price will be 30.59–0.00241 * 13,000 = −0.74 cents! We don't even need to be this extreme, however, to run into negative price forecasts. For instance, a 95% confidence interval given a yield of 7,500 pounds would extend from 12.52 − 2*6.65 to 12.52 + 2*6.65, or from −0.78 to 25.82 cents per pound. Although high yields are likely to drive prices down, negative prices are patently absurd.

Now suppose yields were very low. Our model says that as yield approaches 0, estimated price will not rise above 30.59 cents per pound. Again, this seems absurd. Some restaurants and some premium food stores will be willing to pay much more to be among the few outlets that have avocados available. Thus we might expect prices to soar far above 30 cents per pound in a year when yields are very low.

Finally, we might anticipate a wider confidence interval when yields are low and prices are high than in the opposite situation. If our model gave an estimated price of $1.00 per pound when yields were very low, we might not be surprised to have actual prices differ from the estimate by 20%, from 80 cents to $1.20, for example. By contrast, if the estimated price in a high-yield year were 10 cents, we might still expect actual to differ from estimated price by 20%, but that would result in an interval from 8 to 12 cents, a much narrower interval than in the previous case. However, the regression model that we have used assumes that the residuals are indistinguishable. Therefore confidence limits will be based on the residual standard deviation of 6.65 regardless of the level of yield or the estimated price. Therefore, it cannot take into account our belief that confidence intervals should vary in width, depending on the value of the estimated price.

The simple regression model saying that estimated price = 30.59 − 0.00241 times yield implies that a 1,000 pound increase in yield will decrease price by 2.41 cents, whether we are going from a yield of 1,000 to 2,000 pounds, or from 7,000 to 8,000 pounds. A more satisfactory model might hypothesize that when the yield doubles, price will decrease by some fixed percentage. For example, when yield goes from 1,000 to 2,000 pounds it would have the same percentage effect on price as when it goes from 4,000 to 8,000 pounds. Such a model would also permit confidence intervals to be expressed as percentages of (instead of differences from) estimated price. Models of this sort are called **multiplicative**, as contrasted with the **linear** model we have been considering so far.

Notice that our dissatisfaction with the linear model stems not from lack of fit, or from data that dramatically disagree with assumptions of the model, but from quite theoretical considerations, based primarily on what the model implies for extreme cases. This kind of analysis can be very fruitful in discovering better ways of specifying regression models.

Figures 6.3A and 6.3B once again show the scatter diagram of price vs. yield. Figure 6.3A shows the linear regression estimate and 95% confidence limits. Figure 6.3B shows a multiplicative regression estimate and 95% confidence limits. Both figures have vertical scales that extend beyond the scales in Figures 6.1 and 6.2, but are comparable to one another. In the multiplicative model depicted in Figure 6.3B, notice that low yields result in estimated prices far in excess of 30 cents, that high yields lead to low but positive estimated prices, that the confidence intervals vary in width, and that even for high yields the lower confidence limit is never negative. In the remainder of this chapter we shall discuss how to formulate and interpret multiplicative regression models.

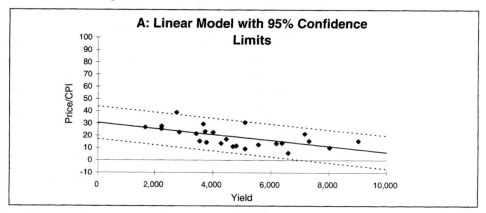

*Figure 6.3A*

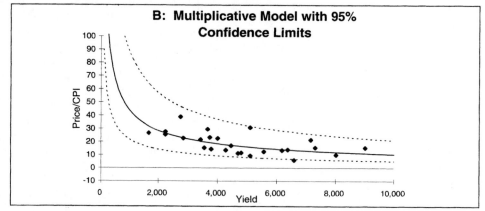

*Figure 6.3B*

# THREE STANDARD
# MULTIPLICATIVE MODELS

There are three cases to consider:

1.  If $x$ is a ratio-scale variable, then as $x$ increases by a fixed *percentage*,[3] $y_{est}$ may increase or decrease by a fixed *amount*. For example, a 1% increase in $x$ might cause $y_{est}$ to increase by 3 units, so that as $x$ went from 100 to 101, or from 500 to 505, or from 2000 to 2020, $y_{est}$ would go up by the same 3 units.

2.  If $y$ is a ratio-scale variable, then as $x$ increases by one unit, $y_{est}$ may increase or decrease by a fixed *percentage*. For instance, a one-unit increase in $x$ might cause $y_{est}$ to increase by 2%. Thus, if $y_{est} = 100$ when $x = 3$ and $y_{est} = 102$ when $x = 4$, this model would imply that $y_{est}$ would go from 682.679 to 696.333 (a 2% increase) when $x$ went from 100 to 101.

---

[3] In all three examples, we assume that if there are other $x$'s included in the model, their values are held constant while we vary the particular $x$ in whose relationship with $y_{est}$ we are interested, and that whatever that relationship is, it does not depend on the values at which the other $x$'s were fixed.

3.  If both $x$ and $y$ are ratio-scale variables, then as $x$ increases by a fixed *percentage*, $y_{est}$ may increase or decrease by a fixed *percentage* as well. By way of example, a one percent increase in $x$ might be accompanied by a 0.5% increase in $y_{est}$. If $y_{est}$ went from 400 to 402 when $x$ went from 100 to 101, this model would imply that $y_{est}$ would go from 1268.54 to 1274.88 (a 0.5% increase) when $x$ went from 1000 to 1010 (a 1% increase).

In what follows we shall look at how to model each of these relationships. Remember that multiplicative relationships can be converted to additive ones by using logarithms (see Chapter 1, *Data Analysis and Statistical Description*), so it should be no surprise that logarithmic transformations will be the key to converting multiplicative models into ones that can be analyzed by regression. The interpretation of the output of such models is tricky, however, and the main point of this chapter is to provide you with such interpretations.

Here are all the mathematical facts you need to know. We shall be dealing with so-called *natural* logarithms (logarithms to the base $e = 2.71828...$). In Excel, you can find the natural logarithm of a number using the = LN function; on most pocket calculators there is an LN key that converts a number to its natural logarithm. If you know the natural logarithm of a number, and want to find the number itself, you use the = EXP function in Excel, or the EXP key on most pocket calculators. Thus, as you should verify, LN(2) = 0.6931, and EXP(0.6931) = 2.

We shall introduce data sets in which one or another of the three models described above is appropriate. While the main purpose of this chapter is to show cases where it makes sense to think of relationships between variables as multiplicative, the particular data sets will give us some opportunity to illustrate some other methodologically useful points as well.

## Model 1: Life Expectancy

We start with an example in which one of the independent variables is clearly measured on a ratio scale, where a plausible model might specify that as it changes by a given multiplicative factor, the estimated value of the dependent variable changes by a given amount.

Data file LIFEXP.XLS shows the life expectancy (in years) and income per capita of people in 101 different countries. The countries are further classified into three categories: industrialized, petroleum exporting, and lesser developed. The data are from 1974;[4] income per capita is given in thousands of 1974 U.S. dollars.

We might start by hypothesizing that income per capita positively affects life expectancy, and test this assumption by performing a regression with life expectancy as the dependent and income per capita as the independent variable. The output of such a regression is shown in Figure 6.4; it suggests that each additional $1,000 of income per capita increases longevity by 6.8 years on the average. The $R^2$ of 0.54 and the high $t$ values may make it seem that this is an adequate model.

---

[4] See Ann Crittenden, "Vital Dialogue Is Beginning Between the Rich and the Poor," *The New York Times*, September 28, 1975, page E-5.

**Regression Number 1**
Dependent Variable: LIFE EXP.

|  | Income/Cap | Constant |
|---|---|---|
| Regr. Coef. | 6.755 | 46.322 |
| Std. Error | 0.627 | 1.101 |
| t value | 10.8 | 42.1 |

| # of obs = | **101** | Deg of F = | **99** |
|---|---|---|---|
| R-squared = | **0.5399** | Resid SD = | **9.018** |

***Figure 6.4***

Do the implications of this model make sense? It's not surprising to find life expectancy going up with income per capita, but wouldn't we expect to find the effect on longevity of going from \$1,000 to \$2,000 per year to be greater than the effect of going from \$4,000 to \$5,000? Indeed, many of the industrialized countries have life expectancies in the 70s. Added income might increase these numbers somewhat, but there are probably diminishing returns. We run up against natural limits that cannot be easily overcome by the benefits that income provides—better medicine, nutrition, shelter, public safety, etc. In those lesser-developed countries with life expectancies in the 20s and 30s, on the other hand, a little additional income per capita might go a long way.

To test the idea of diminishing returns, let's compute values of $y_{est}$ and the residuals, and produce a scatter diagram of these two variables, as shown in Figure 6.5. It indicates that there are no estimated values below 46, even though actual life expectancy was as low as 27. More importantly, the residuals tend to be large positive numbers for estimated life expectancies between about 50 and 70, and to be large negative numbers for very low and very high values of estimated life expectancy. This suggests that actual values of life expectancy exceed estimated values in the middle range, and are less than estimated values at the extremes—an indication of a **curvilinear** [5] relationship between income per capita and life expectancy.[6] According to our diminishing-returns hypothesis, this seems to be a reasonable way for the two variables to be related.

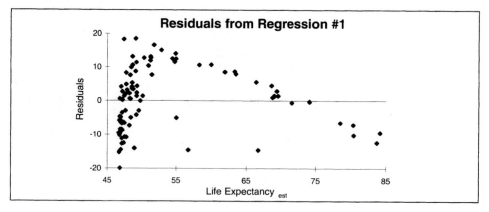

***Figure 6.5***

---

[5] We could try to take account of the curvilinearity by adding as a transformed variable the square of income per capita (see Chapter 4, "Forecasting with Regression Analysis"). But there are other characteristics of the relationship between income per capita and life expectancy that lead us to consider a different transformation.

[6] Had we produced a chart of life expectancy vs. income per capita at the beginning, we would have observed such a relationship, but not in as clear cut form as in Figure 6.5.

Further examination of the file shows that life expectancy ranged from 27 years (in Guinea) to 74.7 years (in Sweden), while income per capita ranged from $50 per year in Mali to $5,596 in Sweden. The ratio of high to low value was less than 3 for life expectancy, but more than 100 for income per capita.

Suppose we now state our diminishing-returns hypothesis more explicitly: a given *percentage* change in income per capita increases life expectancy by a fixed number of years. This implies that doubling income—going from $100 to $200 per year, for example—would result in the same increase in estimated life expectancy as going from $1,000 to $2,000, or from $2,000 to $4,000.

To see whether this hypothesis provides a better explanation of the relationship between the two variables, we must first perform a *logarithmic* transformation (using the = LN function in Excel) of income per capita. Why a logarithmic transformation? Because the *difference* between LN(100) and LN(200) is the same as the difference between LN(1,000) and LN(2,000), or the logarithms of any other number and twice that number. Similarly, differences between the logarithms of pairs of numbers differing by any other multiplicative factor would be the same, i.e., the difference between LN(100) and LN(110) is the same as the difference between LN(1,000) and LN(1,100). If life expectancy increases by the same amount every time income increases by a fixed percentage, it will increase by the same amount every time LN(income) increases by a fixed *amount*.

In Figure 6.6 the output of a regression with life expectancy as the dependent and LN(income per capita) as the independent variable is shown. The fit is clearly better (higher $R^2$), and a plot of the residuals of this regression against the values of $y_{est}$ (Figure 6.7) shows that there is no discernible pattern (although there are a number of large residuals, leading us to wonder whether there are some additional explanatory variables that would account for them).

**Figure 6.6**

| | | LN(inc/cap) | Constant |
|---|---|---|---|
| **Regression Number 2** | | | |
| Dependent Variable: LIFE EXP. | | | |
| Regr. Coef. | | 8.411 | 60.76 |
| Std. Error | | 0.491 | 0.80 |
| t value | | 17.1 | 76.1 |
| | | | |
| # of obs = | **101** | Deg of F = | **99** |
| R-squared = | **0.7474** | Resid SD = | **6.681** |

**Figure 6.7**

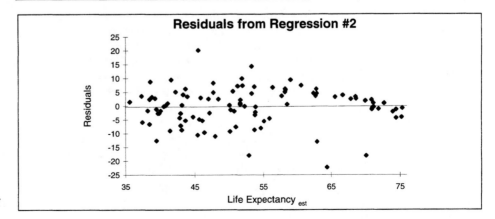

***Interpretation of Output.*** The estimated regression coefficient of 8.411 in Figure 6.6 indicates that as LN(income) increases by one unit, estimated life expectancy goes up by 8.411 years, but that is of little value to a person who wants to understand the relationship of income to life expectancy. What you would like to know is how estimated life expectancy increases as income—not LN(income)—increases by a given percentage. The formula for estimated life expectancy, derived from the output in Figure 6.6, is:

$$y_{est} = 60.76 + 8.411*\text{LN(income)} \, .$$

We can use this formula to compute $y_{est}$ for pairs of values of income that differ by 1%: 100 vs. 101, and 1,000 vs. 1,010. This is done in Table 6.1, which shows estimated life expectancy as a function of per capita income.

**Table 6.1**

| INCOME ($000) | LN(INCOME) | $y_{est}$ |
|---|---|---|
| 0.100 | −2.303 | 41.39 |
| 0.101 | −2.293 | 41.48 |
| 1.000 | 0 | 60.76 |
| 1.010 | 0.00995 | 60.84 |

As income increases from 100 to 101, $y_{est}$ increases from 41.39 to 41.48, an increase of 0.09 years. And as income increases from 1,000 to 1,010, $y_{est}$ increases from 60.76 to 60.84, a difference of 0.08, essentially the same as before except for roundoff error. We conclude that a 1% increase in income is accompanied by a 0.08-year increase in estimated life expectancy. Furthermore, this increase is roughly equal to 1% of the regression coefficient on LN(income). This is not a coincidence. Indeed, in any regression model of the form:

$$y = b_0 + b_1*\text{LN}(x_1) + \ldots + \text{resid} \, ,$$

(where the "+ ... +" indicates that there may be other independent variables besides $x_1$), it can be shown that the effect on $y_{est}$ of increasing $x_1$ by a factor $k$ is $b_1*\text{LN}(k)$; doubling $x_1$, for example, would increase $y_{est}$ by $b_1*\text{LN}(2) = 0.6931b_1$. If $k = 1.01$, representing a 1% increase in $x_1$, the increase in $y_{est}$ is $b_1*\text{LN}(1.01) = 0.00995*b_1$, or approximately $0.01*b_1$. Thus we can approximate the effect on $y_{est}$ of a 1% increase in $x_1$ directly from the regression output, without performing any additional calculations.

***Additional Analysis.*** We noticed a number of large negative residuals in Figure 6.6, and upon scanning the data we see that many of these are associated with countries that are classified as petroleum exporting. Whereas most of the countries in the data base experienced relatively little change in income per capita over the years, the oil exporters experienced a significant jump in 1974 as a result of the OPEC price increase in late 1973. What affects life expectancy is not current income per capita, but rather average income per capita over a sufficiently long period of time to affect the public-health and associated infrastructures. In 1974 income-per-capita of petroleum exporters was probably far above that long-term average. Hence their estimated life expectancy will be too high, giving rise to negative residuals.

In Figure 6.8 we show the results of a regression having as independent variables, in addition to LN(income), two dummy variables representing lesser-developed countries and industrialized countries (petroleum exporters are the base case). The regression coefficients for the two dummies, compared with the base case, are positive (the regression "corrects" for oil exporters' estimated life expectancy being too high), although the difference between the regression coefficients for LDCs and industrialized countries is not sufficiently great to warrant putting them in separate categories. In addition, the $R^2$ is higher, and the RSD is lower: the additional analysis was clearly worthwhile.

**Regression Number 3**
Dependent Variable: LIFE EXP.

|  | LN(inc/cap) | Constant | Devel | LDC |
|---|---|---|---|---|
| Regr. Coef. | 8.810 | 54.25 | 6.647 | 7.770 |
| Std. Error | 0.753 | 2.16 | 2.887 | 2.384 |
| t value | 11.7 | 25.1 | 2.3 | 3.3 |

| # of obs = | **101** | Deg of F = | **97** |
|---|---|---|---|
| R-squared = | **0.7734** | Resid SD = | **6.393** |

*Figure 6.8*

## Model 2: Smoking and Death Rates

Figure 6.9 shows death rates for men as a function of age and smoking behavior, results derived from SMOKING.XLS. A similar chart could be produced for women. As we move from one five-year age bracket to another, the death rate goes up at an increasing rate in every smoking category. Does that mean, in this case, that the death rate goes up by a constant multiplicative factor as we go from one age group to the next? How does the rate go up as degree of inhalation increases? And how is the rate affected by gender?

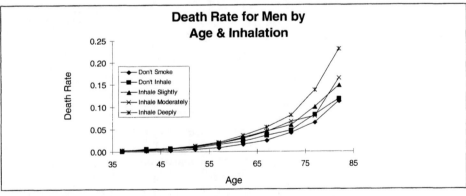

*Figure 6.9*

To answer these questions, we must first rearrange the data so that each age/inhalation/gender category represents an observation. If we code age using the midpoint of each bracket (37, 42, ... , 82), code inhalation as 0 for don't smoke up to 4 for deeply inhale, and code gender as 0 for men, 1 for women, we can create a four-column array of 100 observations. Column 1 contains death rates, and the other three columns contain coded values of age, inhalation, and gender. For convenience, that rearrangement has been performed in data file SMOKINGX.XLS.

If we believe that the effects of the independent variables on death rate are multiplicative, then the effects on the logarithm of death rate should be additive, in the sense that each five-year step in age should add a given amount to LN(death rate), and each increment in severity of inhalation should likewise add a certain amount. If the amounts added are the same for all age increments, or for all inhalation levels, the effects of these variables on LN(death rate) would be linear.

Figure 6.10 shows LN(death rate) as a function of age for men and women and the different levels of inhalation. Although no attempt is made to label the various "curves," it is quite clear that, except in a few instances (primarily cases where death rate is based on very few deaths and thus subject to considerable sampling error), the relationships are very close to linear.

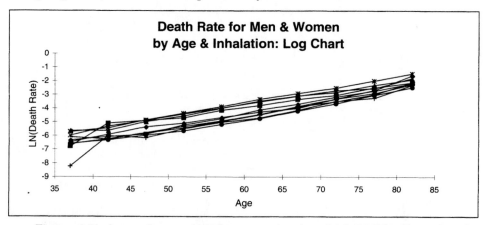

***Figure 6.10***

Figure 6.11 shows the results of a regression in which LN(death rate) is the dependent variable and age, inhalation, and gender are the independent variables. The $R^2$ is remarkably high (0.9710).

**Regression Number 1**
Dependent Variable: LN(DEATH RATE)

|  | Inhalation | Gender (M=0) | Age | Constant |
|---|---|---|---|---|
| Regr. Coef. | 0.1484 | (0.6724) | 0.09462 | (9.882) |
| Std. Error | 0.0177 | 0.0500 | 0.00174 | 0.115 |
| t value | 8.4 | (13.4) | 54.3 | (85.9) |

| | | | |
|---|---|---|---|
| # of obs = | **100** | Deg of F = | **96** |
| R-squared = | **0.9709** | Resid SD = | **0.2501** |

***Figure 6.11***

***Interpretation of Outputs.*** How do the various independent variables affect estimated death rate? From Figure 6.11, a one-year increase in age increases estimated LN(death rate) by 0.0946. Therefore, estimated death rate is increased by a factor of EXP(0.0946) = 1.099, i.e., by about 10% for each additional year of age. In a similar manner, each level of additional inhalation increases death rate by about 15%. The fact that a one-unit increase in $x_1$ increases $y_{est}$ by a factor EXP($b_1$) is true whether $x_1$ is a more-or-less continuous variable, like age, or a dummy variable, like gender. Thus the death rate for women is less than that for men by a factor of EXP(–0.6724) = 0.5105: the death rate for women is only around 50% of that for men of similar age and smoking behavior.

***Additional Analysis.*** The linearity of LN(death rate) with respect to age is apparent from Figure 6.10, but are we justified in assuming that the ordinal variable that represents levels of inhalation causes estimated death rate to go up by roughly equal multiplicative increments? To answer this question, we created five dummy variables, each representing one of the levels of inhalation. Treating "don't smoke" as the base case, we replaced the "inhalation" variable with the other four dummies. The results of the regression are shown in

Figure 6.12. We see that the $R^2$ is very slightly improved and that the RSD is very slightly decreased. The regression coefficients for the dummy variables are plotted in Figure 6.13, and the straight-line relationship implied by the regression of Figure 6.11 is also shown. The "effects" of each additional level of inhalation do not increase in exactly equal steps, but they are not much different from the "effects" implied by the linear model of Figure 6.11. The slightly better fit hardly justifies the added complexity of description. Here is a case where an ordinal variable can be treated as if it were a difference-scale variable.

**Regression Number 2**
Dependent Variable: LN(DEATH RATE)

|  | Gender (M=0) | Age | Constant | | Don't Inhale | Inhale Slightly | Inhale Mod. | Inhale Deeply |
|---|---|---|---|---|---|---|---|---|
| Regr. Coef. | (0.6724) | 0.09462 | (9.897) | | 0.1397 | 0.4033 | 0.4060 | 0.6086 |
| Std. Error | 0.0498 | 0.00173 | 0.120 | | 0.0787 | 0.0787 | 0.0787 | 0.0787 |
| t value | (13.5) | 54.6 | (82.6) | | 1.8 | 5.1 | 5.2 | 7.7 |

| | | | | | |
|---|---|---|---|---|---|
| # of obs = | **100** | Deg of F = | **93** | | |
| R-squared = | **0.9721** | Resid SD = | **0.2490** | | |

*Figure 6.12*

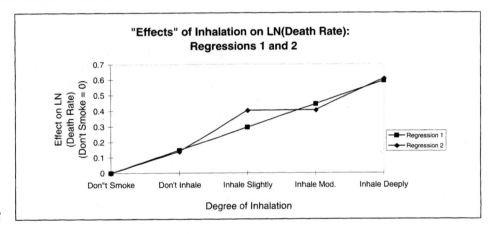

*Figure 6.13*

## Model 3: Avocado Prices

We now return to a more complete discussion of avocado prices. Data file SUNRANCH.XLS contains data on California avocado prices,[7] production, and yield per acre, as well as disposable personal income, U.S. population, and the consumer price index from 1950 through 1974. Using these data, how can we forecast 1975 avocado prices?

California accounted for about 80% of the avocados produced in the U.S. in 1974. Newly planted avocado trees take about five years until they bear fruit. Yield per acre varies quite unpredictably from year to year, so that there are wide swings in production volume. Between 1950 and 1974 growers would increase their acreage when avocado prices were high; ultimately the increased supply of avocados would drive the price down, but better distribution procedures and heavy trade promotion would create sufficient demand to drive prices up again. Figure 6.14 shows prices and production as a function of time.

---

[7] Prices are in cents per pound, production in millions of pounds (for California only), disposable income in billions of dollars, yield in pounds per bearing acre, population in millions, and CPI is scaled so 1967=100%. Data from *Sun Ranch*, Harvard Business School case 9-185-076, by Professor Richard F. Meyer. Reproduced with permission.

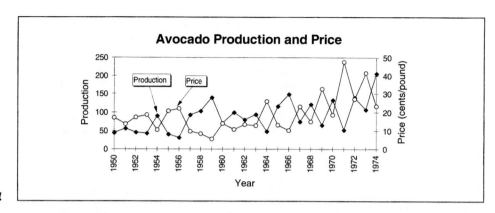

**Figure 6.14**

Figure 6.15 shows the output of a regression in which price was the dependent variable and production, income per capita (income divided by population) and population were the independent variables.[8] The high $R^2$ indicates a very good fit to the data. Yet the model implies that if production increased to 321.4 (millions of) pounds (quite far outside the range of the data, but not inconceivable if enough additional acres were planted and yields remained high), while income and population remained at 1974 levels, a point forecast of the price would be negative, and a 95% confidence interval on forecast price would include negative values even if production were only 301 million pounds. Furthermore, a plot of the residuals of this regression against $y_{est}$ (Figure 6.16) shows that for values of $y_{est}$ in the middle of its range the residuals tend to be negative, while for values of $y_{est}$ at either extreme, the residuals tend to be positive: the model underestimates price for extreme values of $y_{est}$.

**Regression Number 1**
Dependent Variable: PRICE

|              | Constant | Pdtn     |          | Pop      | Inc/Cap |
| ------------ | -------- | -------- | -------- | -------- | ------- |
| Regr. Coef.  | 25.25    | (0.2129) |          | (0.1319) | 15.67   |
| Std. Error   | 8.34     | 0.0132   |          | 0.0589   | 1.23    |
| t value      | 3.0      | (16.1)   |          | (2.2)    | 12.7    |

|                |        |            |       |
| -------------- | ------ | ---------- | ----- |
| # of obs =     | **25** | Deg of F = | **21** |
| R-squared =    | **0.9594** | Resid SD = | **2.184** |

**Figure 6.15**

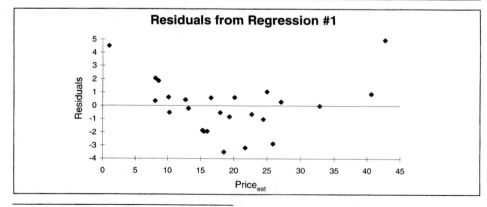

**Figure 6.16**

[8] Notice that we do not, in this or the next model, express price in constant cents (as we did in the introduction to this chapter). We expect any inflationary effects to be captured by the independent variable income per capita.

All of the variables in the model are ratio-scale variables, and a model that hypothesizes *percentage* changes in the independent variables causing *percentage* changes in $y_{est}$ might make more sense; at least there would be no way for forecast values of price to be negative. In Figure 6.17 we show the results of a regression in which logarithms of all the variables are used. The fit as measured by $R^2$ is very slightly worse, but this time an examination of a scatter plot of residuals against values of $y_{est}$ shows essentially random scatter. Even though the $R^2$ is not quite as high as in the nonlogarithmic model, this one is more satisfactory overall.

***Interpretation of Outputs.***   In a model where:

$$LN(y) = b_0 + b_1 * LN(x_1) + \ldots + resid$$

it can be shown that an increase in $x_1$ by a factor $k$ causes $y_{est}$ [the estimated value of $y$, not of $LN(y)$] to change by a factor $k^{b_1}$; for example, doubling $x_1$ will change $y_{est}$ by a factor $2^{b_1}$. If $k = 1.01$, representing a 1% increase in the value of $x_1$, $y_{est}$ will change by a factor $1.01^{b_1}$. To a good approximation, if $b_1$ is between $-5$ and $+5$, a 1% increase in $x_1$ will cause $y_{est}$ to change by $b_1$%. For example, using the regression of Figure 6.17, suppose we hold income and population constant at the 1974 levels of 984.6 and 215.47 respectively, so that income per capita is $984.6/215.47 = 4.5695$, then ask what would happen to estimated price if production increased from its 1974 level of 207 to 209.07, a 1% increase. From the regression coefficients,

**Figure 6.17**

| | | | | Constant | LN(Pdtn) | LN(Inc/Cap) | LN(Pop) |
|---|---|---|---|---|---|---|---|
| **Regression Number 2** | | | | | | | |
| Dependent Variable: LN(PRICE) | | | | | | | |
| Regr. Coef. | | | | 20.36 | (0.9280) | 2.351 | (2.942) |
| Std. Error | | | | 3.60 | 0.0578 | 0.207 | 0.730 |
| t value | | | | 5.7 | (16.1) | 11.4 | (4.0) |
| # of obs = | **25** | Deg of F = | **21** | | | | |
| R-squared = | **0.9589** | Resid SD = | **0.1094** | | | | |

$$
\begin{aligned}
LN(price)_{est} &= 20.36 - 0.9280 * LN(production) \\
&\quad + 2.351 * LN(4.5695) \\
&\quad - 2.942 * LN(215.47) \\
&= 8.1253 - 0.9280 * LN(production) \, .
\end{aligned}
$$

Table 6.2 shows estimated price for production levels of 207 and 209.07:

**Table 6.2**

| PRODUCTION | LN(PRODUCTION) | LN(PRICE)$_{est}$ | PRICE$_{est}$ |
|---|---|---|---|
| 207.0 | 5.3327 | 3.17655 | 23.964 |
| 209.07 | 5.3427 | 3.16727 | 23.743 |

As we can see, a 1% increase in production caused a change in price of $(23.743 - 23.964)/23.964 = -0.922\%$: $-0.922$ is approximately equal in value to $b_1$.[9]

*Forecasts.*    In a regression model involving a logarithmic transformation of the dependent variable, point forecasts can be computed by the method we have just used. To express forecast uncertainty in the form of a confidence interval, you can first compute a lower and upper confidence limit for $LN(y)$, and then compute EXP of these limits to obtain similar limits for $y$ itself. For example, we have already seen that the point forecast for $LN(price)$ based on income per capita of 4.5695, population of 215.47, and production of 207 is 3.17655. A 95% confidence interval for $LN(price)$ has a lower limit of $3.17655 - 2*0.1094 = 2.9578$ and an upper limit of $3.17655 + 2*0.1094 = 3.3954$, where 0.1094 is the value of the RSD in the regression of Figure 6.17. From these results, the 95% confidence limit for price extends from $EXP(2.9578) = 19.26$ to $EXP(3.3954) = 29.83$. (Remember that this interval, like all intervals derived in this way from regression output, is too narrow; in particular, it assumes that we know production for 1975, which depends on yield, and yield has been very hard to forecast in the past.) Because values computed using the EXP function are necessarily positive, a nice consequence of this analysis is that no confidence interval covers a negative price.

# SUMMARY

The three models we have considered in this chapter are

$$y = b_0 + b_1 LN(x_1) + \dots + resid , \qquad \text{(Model 1)},$$

$$LN(y) = b_0 + b_1 x_1 + \dots + resid , \qquad \text{(Model 2)},$$

and

$$LN(y) = b_0 + b_1 LN(x_1) + \dots + resid . \qquad \text{(Model 3)}.$$

Model 1 was used to represent the relationship between life expectancy and income per capita in a sample of 101 countries; Model 2 to represent the relationship between death rates and age, smoking behavior, and gender in a sample of 1,000,000 adults; and Model 3 to represent the relationship between avocado prices and production, income per capita, and population in a sample of 25 years.

In Model 1, if $x_1$ increases by a *factor k*, $y_{est}$ changes by $b_1 LN(k)$ *units*; if $x_1$ increases by 1%, $y_{est}$ changes by approximately $0.01 b_1$ units.

In Model 2, if $x_1$ increases by one unit, $y_{est}$ changes by a *factor* $EXP(b_1)$. If $b_1$ is between $-0.2$ and $+0.2$, $y_{est}$ changes by a factor of approximately $1 + b_1$, or $100 b_1\%$.

In Model 3, if $x_1$ increases by a factor $k$, $y_{est}$ changes by a factor $k^{b_1}$; if $x_1$ increases by 1%, $y_{est}$ changes by a factor of approximately $1 + 0.01 b_1$, or $b_1\%$.

---

[9] Economists call the percentage change in one variable that accompanies a 1% change in another variable an **elasticity**. They usually look at how quantity demanded or supplied varies with price or other factors. Here we are looking at it the other way: how does price vary with quantity supplied (production) and other factors? Because the percentage change in price for a 1% change in production is $-0.922\%$, whether production changes from 100 to 101 or from 300 to 303, a regression model in which both the dependent variable and the independent variables are expressed in logarithmic form (Model 3) is said to be a **constant-elasticity** model.

# EXERCISE

Data file TIO2.XLS contains cost, capacity, and output data about DuPont's titanium dioxide business from 1955 through 1970. The standard learning-curve model asserts that every 1% increase in cumulative output will be accompanied by a constant percent decrease in unit manufacturing cost (measured in real, not nominal, dollars). For example, if manufacturing cost of an item were $100 when cumulative output was 1,000, the cost might drop to $99.50 (a 0.5% drop) when cumulative output increased to 1,010, and if this were so, we might expect a 0.5% drop in cost (in real terms) when cumulative output went from 2,000 to 2,020.

1. Use the data in file TIO2.XLS to see whether the manufacturing cost of titanium dioxide followed such a learning curve. If so, estimate by how much real costs decreased for each 1% increase in cumulative output. By how much did they decrease when cumulative output doubled?

2. In addition to learning effects, manufacturing costs are also influenced by economies of scale and capacity utilization. Scale is often measured in terms of plant capacity; from the data available, we can compute average plant capacity by dividing total capacity by the number of plants. Capacity utilization is simply the output in a given year divided by the capacity available in that year, usually expressed as a percent. Develop a model that relates cost to cumulative output, scale, and capacity utilization. Interpret the results of your model.

# INDEX

*References to footnotes are indicated by the page number followed by a lowercase n.*

There is a natural tendency to assume that the best way to manage a risk is by reducing it or eliminating it. Not all risks are bad. In this chapter we examine the potential for risks to "average out" when viewed as a portfolio. The portfolio view of risk is fundamental to the development in this book. We begin with a motivational case, followed by a note and exercises that will establish and explain the concepts involved.

## CASE    BREAKFAST FOODS CORPORATION

John Morgan, CEO of Breakfast Foods Corporation (BF, makers of "Wheatflakes" and others), had just come back to his office from lunch when the phone rang to announce Ron Sykes, his marketing VP:

"John, I told our sales force to keep their ears to the ground regarding any possible move by MC (Morning Cereal, Inc., BF's principal competitor) to start a price war. They are just crazy enough to do that even though it would hurt both of us. I told the sales force that if a price war is going to happen, it's an enormous advantage to be the first one to start. So we wanted to know the minute there are signs that MC is ready to move. Well, Fred Sharp called me fifteen minutes ago. He has a contact inside one of the major networks who tells him that MC has just booked large blocks of advertising space starting two weeks from today. Now you and I know that there's no way MC wants big blocks of advertising space unless they're announcing price reductions."

"Ron, how sure are you that Sharp is reliable as a source? We wouldn't want to jump to hasty conclusions."

"Well, normally I wouldn't pay much attention to a report like this except that Fred reminded me, with some acerbity I thought, of three previous occasions when he correctly called a major move by MC. I checked the files and, indeed, he had given us significant information before those three occasions. John, I think we should take this seriously and beat them to the punch."

"O.K., Ron, bring me a proposal before six o'clock."

John turned to a report on his desk from David Baker, a recent graduate of the Stanford Business School whom John had hired as a general assistant. This report concerned John's desire to fire one of BF's three wheat price forecasters. Every three months, for nearly ten years, BF had received from these men best-guess forecasts of wheat prices three months hence as part of BF's desire to reduce its purchase costs. BF relied exclusively on these forecasts since the experts had already assimilated information from such sources as futures prices, econometric models, and so on.

Harvard Business School case 9-182-202. This case was prepared by Professor David E. Bell. The first of the two issues in this case is adapted from an example in *Judgement and Choice*, by R.M. Hogarth, John Wiley & Sons, 1980. Copyright © 1982 by the President and Fellows of Harvard College.

However, their ten-year tenure had led the experts to be overly exacting in their demands for retaining fees, and John felt that firing one of them would not only cut costs directly by about a third, but indirectly it would send the message to the remaining two that no one was indispensable. He had asked David to evaluate which one should get his marching orders.

David's memo read as follows:

> I dug out the forecasts made by our three experts and compared them with the actual prices that resulted three months later (Exhibit 1). I plotted a distribution of errors for each of them (Exhibit 2). Clearly what we want is to fire the expert with the widest spread (variance) of errors. The graph shows that this is Harry.

## Exhibit 1

### ERROR (ACTUAL PRICE — FORECAST PRICE TO NEAREST CENT/BUSHEL)

| Forecast # | Tom Smith | Dick Wilson | Harry Simpson |
|---|---|---|---|
| 1 | –3 | –3 | 23 |
| 2 | –13 | –4 | 22 |
| 3 | 5 | 7 | 1 |
| 4 | 13 | 0 | –16 |
| 5 | 5 | –4 | –31 |
| 6 | 4 | 2 | 1 |
| 7 | –4 | 6 | 11 |
| 8 | –13 | 6 | 36 |
| 9 | –8 | –7 | –5 |
| 10 | 0 | 5 | 1 |
| 11 | 0 | 4 | –2 |
| 12 | 5 | 8 | –24 |
| 13 | 1 | –4 | 15 |
| 14 | –6 | –10 | 15 |
| 15 | –13 | –15 | 11 |
| 16 | 3 | 3 | 3 |
| 17 | 2 | 3 | –10 |
| 18 | 7 | 0 | –6 |
| 19 | –1 | –3 | –5 |
| 20 | –4 | –4 | 17 |
| 21 | 4 | –8 | –25 |
| 22 | 2 | 0 | –19 |
| 23 | 0 | 3 | –9 |
| 24 | –5 | –12 | 7 |
| 25 | 1 | 8 | 0 |
| 26 | –10 | –9 | 11 |
| 27 | –7 | 0 | 21 |
| 28 | –3 | 3 | 33 |
| 29 | 2 | –4 | –22 |
| 30 | 2 | 4 | –12 |
| 31 | –3 | –4 | 12 |
| 32 | 10 | 0 | –41 |
| 33 | –10 | –12 | 9 |
| 34 | 8 | 19 | –17 |
| 35 | –8 | 6 | 8 |
| 36 | 2 | –7 | –6 |
| 37 | –3 | –10 | –10 |
| 38 | 2 | 6 | –4 |
| 39 | –8 | –13 | –6 |
| 40 | 3 | 2 | –12 |

## A Month Later

John read two memos on his desk. The first was from Ron Sykes:

> We should really give Fred Sharp some kind of bonus or recognition. As you recall he was the one that told us about MC's booking of advertising space two weeks before we would have seen it for ourselves on TV. Because of him we beat them to the punch. What do you think?

The second memo was from David Baker:

> I thought you'd be amused to hear that Harry Simpson has been retained by MC as part of their forecasting team. Not only did we get rid of him, MC actually hired him. Let's hope they're paying him some outrageous salary.

## Exhibit 2

### DISTRIBUTION OF ERRORS

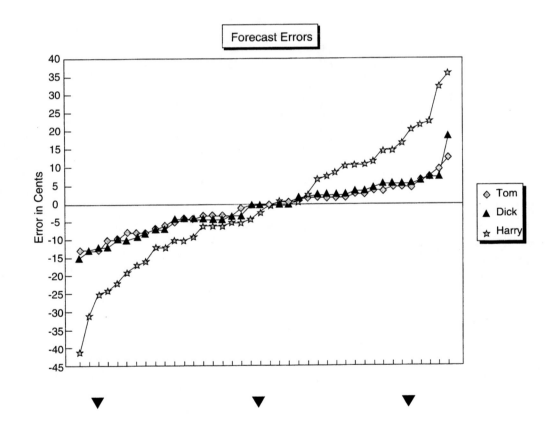